The Politics of Northern Ireland

D1389276

Books in the Politics Study Guides series

The Politics of Northern Ireland

Joanne McEvoy

Edinburgh University Press

Joanne McEvoy, 2008

Edinburgh University Press Ltd
22 George Square, Edinburgh

Typeset in 11/13pt Monotype Baskerville by
Servis Filmsetting Ltd, Manchester, and
printed and bound in Great Britain by
GraphyCems, Spain

A CIP record for this book is available from the British Library

ISBN 978 0 7486 2501 7 (paperback)

The right of Joanne McEvoy to be identified as author of this work has been
asserted in accordance with the Copyright, Designs and Patents Act 1988.

Published with the support of the Edinburgh University Scholarly Publishing Initiatives
Fund.

Contents

Boxes

Tables

Introduction

The Northern Ireland conflict, known locally as 'the Troubles', endured for three decades and claimed the lives of more than 3,500 people. The conflict also resulted in thousands of people being injured, bereaved or victimised because they were from the 'other side' or simply in the wrong place at the wrong time. For many years the violence continued with little potential for resolution as none of the political initiatives advanced from the 1970s to the late 1990s satisfied both nationalists and unionists.

In what became known as the Northern Ireland 'peace process', politics in the region was transformed in the 1990s due to a set of changed political circumstances: most notably the signals of change within the republican movement and the IRA ceasefires of 1994 and 1997. Multi-party negotiations finally led to a political settlement agreed among (most) political parties on Good Friday, 10 April 1998.[1] The 'historic' Agreement established a set of new political institutions: internal power-sharing government between nationalists, unionists and republicans; and structures to reflect the important north–south and east–west relations. Following the transfer of power from Westminster to the Northern Ireland Assembly on 2 December 1999, a new administration with local ministers began to govern the region together. The Assembly operated intermittently with suspensions arising from the issue of IRA decommissioning and was suspended for the fourth and final time on 14 October 2002.

Considerable stalemate ensued in the aftermath of suspension as the British and Irish Governments attempted to reach agreement among the parties; a particular challenge following the Democratic Unionist Party (DUP) and Sinn Féin successes at the 2003 Northern Ireland Assembly election. In 2006 the two governments produced the St Andrews Agreement with a timetable for the restoration of devolved power sharing. The new agreement was accepted by the parties and led to a series of historic political developments including Sinn Féin's support for the Police Service of Northern Ireland and the DUP's willingness to share power with republicans. Agreement between the two main parties led to the formation of a new coalition on 8 May 2007. Power was then transferred to the Northern Ireland Assembly and the third devolved power-sharing government in Northern Ireland in more than 30 years. Local ministers were once again charged with taking decisions on policy issues in the hope of more 'normal' politics embedding in the region.

Chapter outline

The objective of this book is to provide an up-to-date and comprehensive introduction to the politics of Northern Ireland from the outbreak of 'the Troubles' in the late 1960s to the restoration of devolution in 2007. It has been written to present the key material in an accessible manner, particularly for students of Northern Ireland politics, UK politics, or peace and conflict studies.

Chapter 1 presents the theoretical perspectives relating to the conflict in Northern Ireland. It seeks to explain the conflict as being ethno-national in nature where two ethnic groups seek national self-determination. While nationalists, who consider themselves Irish, mostly aspire to a united Ireland, unionists uphold their Britishness and want Northern Ireland to remain within the United Kingdom. Identity is, therefore, a central feature of political life in Northern Ireland. While a sizeable proportion of the population profess to be neither nationalist nor unionist, this is not borne out at the polls as the ethnic parties continue to dominate. The chapter does, however, point to the debate in the academic literature which argues for a move beyond the 'two communities' model and recognise the internal divisions within nationalism and unionism and the overlapping layers of identity.

Chapter 1 then presents the literature relating to Marxist accounts of the conflict which, although no longer dominant, are interesting in their efforts to develop a class analysis of the divisions in the interests of the working class. Another perspective, the colonial interpretation, which has been held by republicans, argues that the conflict was a consequence of the colonisation of Ireland by Britain. This perspective suggested that British withdrawal would bring the conflict to an end. In keeping with theory, the chapter introduces consociationalism, a theory of power sharing in divided societies. The main principle of consociational theory is the 'grand coalition' whereby representatives of the main segments in society cooperate in a coalition government.

Chapter 2 explores the historical context of the conflict which led to the onset of sectarian violence at the end of the 1960s. It traces the roots of division from the Anglo-Norman invasion of 1169 and the Plantations of the sixteenth and seventeenth centuries, when the native Gaelic Irish were dispossessed of their land which was given to the Scots and English settlers. Under the Penal Laws Catholics were excluded from the political establishment and subject to harsh measures, including being banned from owning property, and Catholic schools and burials were made illegal. A revolutionary movement, the United Irishmen staged a (failed) rebellion in 1798. Under the Act of Union 1801 the Irish parliament was formally integrated into the parliament of Great Britain.

Chapter 2 also traces the Home Rule movement leading to the Government of Ireland Act 1920 which created two jurisdictions and two parliaments, one in Dublin and one in Belfast. The Anglo-Irish Treaty 1921 then provided for Irish independence in the Irish Free State while Northern Ireland remained within the UK. The birth of Northern Ireland led to 50 years of unionist control until the introduction of direct rule from Westminster in 1972. The system discriminated against the Catholic minority in relation to the electoral system, gerrymandering, housing allocation and employment. By the mid-1960s, a civil rights campaign was formed which contributed to the downfall of Stormont. Amid sectarian violence and the re-emergence of the Irish Republican Army (IRA), 'the Troubles' broke out at the end of the 1960s, triggering much violence in the early 1970s and lasting until the end of the 1990s. Finally, the chapter looks at the extent of communal divisions in Northern Ireland in relation to education, culture and sport and residential segregation.

Chapter 3 explores the positions of the various political parties as well as the rationale for violence on the part of republican and loyalist paramilitaries. It looks at the main parties in turn: the Ulster Unionist Party; the Democratic Unionist Party; the Social Democratic and Labour Party; Sinn Féin; the Alliance Party of Northern Ireland; and the Progressive Unionist Party. It discusses the parties' positions in relation to Northern Ireland's constitutional status and their respective contributions to the 'peace process'. The chapter then turns to explore republican and loyalist paramilitaries and their respective rationale for using violence. It also discusses the contentious issue of the decommissioning of weapons and ammunition held by the paramilitaries.

Chapter 4 turns to explore the attempts made to resolve the conflict in the form of political initiatives from the 1970s to the mid-1990s. Following the introduction of direct rule in 1972, the inter-party talks at Sunningdale produced an agreement and the formation of a power-sharing government. The Executive was not to last, however, principally due to the extent of intra-unionist divisions over power sharing and, in particular, the proposed Council of Ireland. The Ulster workers' strike put the final nail in the coffin and led to the resignation of the government's chief executive, Brian Faulkner, and the collapse of the Executive. The chapter then charts the different proposals over the years designed to produce agreement between unionists and nationalists: the 'Rolling Devolution' plan of 1982; the Anglo-Irish Agreement of 1985; the Brooke–Mayhew talks of 1991–2; the Downing Street Declaration of 1993; and the Framework Documents of 1995. Ultimately, none of these initiatives satisfied both nationalists and unionists. While the Social Democratic and Labour Party (SDLP) was adamant that new political structures necessitated an 'Irish dimension' and internal power sharing, unionists resisted coalition government and were strongly opposed to the Irish Republic having a say in the affairs of Northern Ireland.

The crucial role played by the British and Irish Governments in the 'peace process' is discussed in Chapter 5. The chapter explores the relationship of the two governments with unionism and nationalism, respectively. It considers the question of whether the British Government can be said to be a cause of the conflict or a neutral arbiter. The British Government's relationship with republicanism has been central to finding a solution; from the secret back-channel talks of the early 1990s to the decision to include Sinn Féin in inter-party talks in 1997. The chapter looks at the role of the Irish Government in the 'peace process', its relationship with unionism and the so-called 'Pan-Nationalist Front'. The partnership between the two governments and the 'convergence' of their positions are considered, particularly in relation to the 1998 Agreement and efforts to restore devolution following suspension of the institutions in October 2002.

Chapter 6 focuses on the unfolding 'peace process' of the 1990s leading to the signing of the Good Friday/Belfast Agreement in 1998.

It explores the multi-party talks including republicans and the contentious issue of IRA decommissioning. The chapter presents the reasons why the deal was deemed 'historic' and its significance in including Sinn Féin and promising an end to paramilitary violence. It then discusses the results of the referendum on the Agreement in May 1998 and the June Northern Ireland Assembly election. Importantly, the chapter outlines why some parties supported the Agreement and why others opposed it. Moreover, it was supported by parties for different reasons: the Trimble camp within the Ulster Unionist Party (UUP) and the loyalist parties viewed the Agreement as cementing the Union; the SDLP and Sinn Féin looked to the increased north–south dimension and the institutions as a transitional phase to a united Ireland. The DUP and the United Kingdom Unionist Party (UKUP) were, however, vehemently opposed to the inclusion of Sinn Féin in government prior to IRA decommissioning and were suspicious of the north–south bodies and the North–South Ministerial Council.

The institutional framework of the Agreement and the operation of the Northern Ireland Assembly and Executive from 1999 to 2002 is the focus of Chapter 7. It takes a detailed look at the institutions and their operation until the administration's fourth and final suspension in October 2002. The chapter discusses the major difficulties experienced during devolution including inter-party tensions, the 'half in, half out' position of the DUP and the stalemate over decommissioning. It signals, however, the successes of the administration as evidenced by the developing role of the Assembly Committees and a number of policy initiatives. The chapter then turns to explore the operation of Strand Two (north–south relations) and Strand Three (east–west relations). Following discussion of progress on decommissioning, the chapter considers the contentious issue of police reform whereby the Patten recommendations were difficult for unionists but crucial for nationalists and republicans.

The final chapter explores the political developments following the suspension of the institutions in 2002 and tracks events leading to the formation of the DUP/Sinn Féin-led coalition in May 2007. It begins with a focus on the political stalemate following suspension, results of the 2003 Assembly election and the extent of unionist disaffection with the implementation of the Belfast Agreement. In 2004 the parties were called to Stormont to undertake a Review of the Agreement; some parties published proposed amendments to the Agreement and the British and Irish Governments produced their 'Comprehensive Agreement' proposals in December 2004. In the absence of political progress, inter-party talks were held at St Andrews, Scotland in 2006. The chapter highlights the important amendments to the 1998 Agreement made in the Northern Ireland (St Andrews Agreement) Act 2006. Finally, the chapter charts the political events surrounding the 2007 Assembly election, the agreement between the DUP and Sinn Féin and the restoration of devolved power sharing on 8 May 2007.

A study guide

The book has been written to meet the requirements of students taking courses in the Politics of Northern Ireland, UK Politics and Conflict Resolution. Students will find the book particularly useful as it presents the key information and arguments in an accessible style and format. The book will also be a useful introduction for general readers interested in the politics of Northern Ireland and conflict resolution.

Each chapter includes bullet points under 'key issues to be covered in this chapter'. Boxes and tables are used to highlight key material where appropriate throughout the book. The chapters also provide sample examination questions to help guide students in their exam preparation. In addition, students will benefit from a summary of the main points in each chapter as well as useful websites and some recommendations for further reading.

CHAPTER 1

Theoretical Perspectives on the Northern Ireland Conflict

Contents

Overview

There is an extensive literature on the Northern Ireland conflict encompassing a number of alternative explanations. This chapter seeks to introduce these theoretical approaches and explain the conflict as ethno-national in nature. It shows that the problem needs to be considered as one of opposing identities: unionists look to Britain whereas nationalists look to the Republic of Ireland. The chapter also introduces the concepts of 'ethnicity' and 'identity' as applied to the Northern Ireland context. Following an overview of the main explanations of the conflict, the chapter explores the main theoretical discussions on how the conflict could be resolved. This involves understanding the debates on power sharing as a means to manage ethnic conflict, focusing on the theory of consociationalism and more integrative approaches.

Key issues to be covered in this chapter

- The arguments for understanding the conflict as ethno-national in nature
- The concept of 'ethnicity' and the ethno-national aspirations for self-determination
- The concept of 'identity' on the part of the nationalist and unionist communities
- The recommendation of moving beyond the 'two communities' model to appreciate the wider diversity in Northern Ireland
- The position and critique of Marxist accounts and the colonial interpretation
- The debate between consociationalism and integrative approaches to power-sharing in divided societies

The ethno-national conflict

The conflict in Northern Ireland is often mistaken as being a religious conflict between the Catholic and the Protestant communities. A closer inspection of the nature of the conflict, however, shows that this explanation is misguided. Indeed, the conflict is not *about* religion. Instead, it is about national identity whereby the nationalist community looks to the Republic of Ireland as the 'motherland' whereas the unionist community looks to Britain as their patron state. While nationalists aspire to a united Ireland, unionists hope to maintain Northern Ireland as part of the United Kingdom. The conflict is, therefore, about two groups with allegiances to two different national communities, Britain and Ireland, which themselves have had a long history of conflict.

This brings us to recognise that the conflict is not just about the internal relationships between nationalists and unionists. There is an important external relationship between the British state and the Republic of Ireland as well as between the internal communities and the two external states. For instance, O'Leary and McGarry note the 'endogenous' and 'exogenous' dimensions of the conflict where 'Irish and British nationalism remain locked in a stand-off' as 'the two ethnic communities in Northern Ireland have been mobilized into the Irish and British "nations"'.[1]

Of course, Northern Ireland society does have clear religious divisions which are frequently expressed in terms of religious intolerance and sectarianism. Sectarianism was abundantly clear during 'the Troubles' and remains an issue evidenced by ongoing attacks on places of worship. The religious factor in Northern Ireland arises from the fact that the religious identity of the two communities coincides with the ethno-national divide. Religion is thus the ethnic marker, or fault line, of the conflict. As McGarry and O'Leary note, Protestants and Catholics are 'divided by religion, by definition, but they are also divided by differences in economic and political power, by historical experience, and, most intensely, by national political identity'.[2]

The religious factor arises from the history of the region whereby nationalists are almost exclusively Catholic and unionists are over-whelmingly Protestant. To put this in simple terms, the religious factor goes back to the colonisation of Ireland more than 300 years ago: the 'native' Irish community were Catholic whereas the 'settlers' from

Scotland and England were Protestant. Catholics/nationalists, therefore, identify with the Republic of Ireland whereas the Protestant/unionist community looks to Britain as their 'homeland', wanting Northern Ireland to be maintained within the United Kingdom. Furthermore, just as the nationalist Catholic community identifies with the Republic of Ireland as 'Catholic' and 'Irish', the Protestant community thus feels its identity would be under threat if a united Ireland were to come about; Protestants would be subsumed into an Irish Catholic state where their own religion and traditions would be at stake. That the Irish state has become increasingly secular and liberal in recent years may yet provide little comfort for unionists.

In explaining the conflict in Northern Ireland as 'ethno-national', we need to consider the meaning of '**ethnicity**' and how a group defines its national identity on the basis of ethnicity. An ethnic group is thus one in which its members have a common descent, culture, language and religion which serve as the demarcations of a given community. The members of the ethnic group share a common heritage and memories of past events as well as similar aspirations for their future. It is also important that the group identifies itself as a united, distinct group, is recognised by other groups in this way and in turn identifies other groups as ethnicities based on differences of religion, language and culture.

An ethnic group becomes an ethno-national group when there is an ethnic basis for nationhood. Nationalism becomes a potent force when the group strives for political autonomy and unity on the basis of its identity as a 'nation'. Anthony D. Smith suggests that 'national identity' involves some sense of political community which implies:

> at least some common institutions and a single code of rights and duties for all the members of the community. It also suggests a definite social space, a fairly well demarcated and bounded territory, with which the members identify and to which they feel they belong.[3]

In his major work on **ethno-nationalism**, Walker Connor describes the nation as 'a self-differentiating ethnic group. A prerequisite of nationhood is a popularly held awareness of belief that one's own group is unique in a most vital sense'.[4] Connor argues that the essence of the nation is a matter of attitude and that the cultural cleavages such as language, religion and race contribute to the sense of uniqueness shared by the nation. What matters in ethnic conflict is the 'divergence of basic identity which manifests itself in "us-versus-them" syndrome'.[5]

If we define the unionist and nationalist communities as ethnonational groups and explain the conflict in relation to two opposing nationalist allegiances, it is important to explore the issue as one of self-determination. The principle of self-determination stipulates that a nation has the right to exercise political power in a clear territorial unit. An ethnic group may thus seek political autonomy within the existing state or secede from the state to create a new independent state. The group's reasons for seeking self-determination vary from case to case but principally arise from circumstances in which the group feels unable to exist with other ethnic groups in the same state and may feel alienated and frustrated at being treated as a subordinate and discriminated group. In an ideal situation the territory of the new state will coincide with the ethnic group and there are no ethnic minorities left behind or a new alienated minority within the new state. The principle of self-determination is relevant to Northern Ireland because both communities aspire to self-determination for their respective nations: nationalists seek unification with the Republic of Ireland; and unionists hope to maintain the Union with Britain.

The concept of identity in Northern Ireland

The concept of identity is an important consideration for ethnic groups and their objective of self-determination. In Northern Ireland identity is clearly pertinent to how the conflict has and continues to play out in terms of nationalist versus unionist identification. This section explores how social and cultural forces constitute ethnonationalist identity and how this takes place in Northern Ireland. On the one hand, the unionist community identifies with Britain as its patron state. Their sense of Britishness is expressed *via* social and cultural activities such as the Orange parades and commemoration of the First and Second World Wars which demonstrate their loyalty to the British state and the Crown. On the other hand, nationalist identity focuses on the Gaelic Athletic Association and the Irish language. John Barry notes how the idea of 'loyalty' is bound up with identity: 'The relations that constitute one's loyalty to particular institutions, places and people are constitutive of one's identity and membership of the valued community that shares that loyalty'.[6]

It is often argued, however, that the unionist community's sense of Britishness is not reciprocated by the British state and the British public in general. As Barry notes, this non-reciprocal relationship creates insecurity for unionists:

> Unionist culture and collective identity are problematic to the extent that their sense of 'Britishness' requires some recognition and acknowledgement of this from the British people and the British state. But since this recognition and affirmation is not forthcoming, this leaves the Ulster unionist identity unstable and unsure.[7]

The nationalist community can also be said to have a non-reciprocal relationship with its patron nation-state, the Republic of Ireland, albeit not to the same extent as that experienced between unionism and Britain. Nevertheless, as Barry notes, nationalists in Northern Ireland have experienced 'isolation and abandonment' in relation to the Republic of Ireland.[8] Irish Governments have, of course, supported northern nationalists in their cause to secure equal rights and have championed the objective of power sharing in Northern Ireland.

It is also interesting to note that not everyone in Northern Ireland identifies themselves as unionist or nationalist. This is confirmed in the results of the annual Northern Ireland Life and Times Survey which records the attitudes, values and beliefs of the people of Northern Ireland on a range of social and political issues. The survey illustrates that a significant number of people in Northern Ireland do not consider themselves to fit in readily with either of the two main categories of identification. In response to the question on identity, approximately a third of people surveyed have consistently described themselves as 'neither' nationalist nor unionist. Since the survey started in 1998 the percentage of people describing themselves as 'neither' has been at its lowest (30 per cent) in 1999 and at its highest (40 per cent) in 2006 (see www.ark.ac.uk/nilt).

It would also seem appropriate not to treat nationalism and unionism as two great monoliths which harbour homogeneous communities. Indeed, there are a number of divergent attitudes and standpoints expressed within both traditions which will be explored more fully in a later chapter. It is important at this stage, however, to introduce some of the arguments which suggest that the conflict should move beyond a 'two communities' model. A number of scholars maintain that the explanation of the conflict in Northern Ireland as simply to do with two opposing nationalisms does not appreciate fully the complexity of the problem and the internal divisions within nationalism and unionism.

Adrian Little says that the debates on the Northern Ireland conflict 'need to move beyond constructed binary divisions and accommodate a much wider understanding of difference'.[9] According to Little the 'two communities' model 'militated against the development of a broader multiculturalism, simplified the diversity that exists within Northern Ireland, and failed to grasp the diversity that exists within each of the "two communities"'.[10] Little discusses the potential for change within the two communities in the context of individuals' changing circumstances and conflict within communities. He suggests that internal relations are 'dynamic in themselves and will vary according to a range of political, social, economic and cultural factors' and refers to the cross-cutting sources of identity based on geographical location and social class.[11]

The nationalist/unionist dichotomy is, therefore, somewhat over-simplified and ignores the exclusion of some groups who do not fit easily into the two main categories and fails to appreciate the overlapping layers of national identity. For instance, in thinking about the theorisation of nationalism and ethnicity we also need to recognise the ways in which ethno-nationalism is gendered. The gendered character of nationalism and ethnicity is clear in the context of a divided society, where violence, conflict and the state are associated with 'masculinity' and 'femininity' is associated with the private domain, the home and domesticity. Women are regarded as the home-makers and in need of protection from the other 'side' in the conflict. Nationality and ethnicity, therefore, construct gendered identities.[12]

Because ethno-nationalism involves processes of exclusion and inclusion in terms of the 'us versus them' scenario, it is important not to overlook the exclusion of groups such as women and ethnic minorities. Elisabeth Porter advances the view that there is a need for a plural acceptance of 'identities of nationality' to bring about peace and inclusivity in Northern Ireland. She suggests that viewing the conflict as one between nationalists and unionists has three shortcomings: 'it oversimplifies national identity, it fails to recognise that unionism is also a form of nationalism and it silences the extent to which nationalism is thoroughly gendered'.[13] We need to take account of the crossovers and interaction between people, such as cross-community marriages and relationships, experiences in the labour market, education, geography and class which all call into question the simple nationalist/unionist dichotomy.

Thus, there exists the view that national identity in Northern Ireland is not as clear-cut as it might first appear. The changing circumstances and the complexity of the problem can be found in surveys on how people express their preference for Northern Ireland's future constitutional status. For instance, 20 per cent of Catholics surveyed for the Northern Ireland Life and Times Survey in 2002 said that Northern Ireland should not unify with the Republic of Ireland (58 per cent of Catholics said it should, 3 per cent of Protestants said it should and 83 per cent of Protestants said it should not). The 2004 survey asked respondents what the long-term policy for Northern Ireland's constitutional future should be and, interestingly, 24 per cent of Catholics said Northern Ireland should remain part of UK, 47 per cent of Catholics would support a united Ireland and 15 per cent of Catholics would prefer an independent state. To the same question 85 per cent of Protestants responded that Northern Ireland should remain part of UK, 5 per cent said it should reunify with the Republic of Ireland and 6 per cent said they would support an independent state.

These statistics suggest that the situation is not as well defined as might first be thought. We need to appreciate the complexity of positions, the potential for shifts in attitude within the two major traditions and the cross-overs between the two communities expressed by people who cannot be assigned easily into a pre-defined category of nationalist or unionist. As Porter writes, the Catholic nationalist and Protestant unionist oppositions 'ignore the complex nature of identity formed through overlapping relationships of race, ethnicity, class, gender, religion, family and national identifications'.[14] At the same time, however, recognition of complexity should not take away from the main issue which is the unresolved problem of how to accommodate two competing nationalisms. As McGarry and O'Leary note, not everyone in Northern Ireland is an 'uncompromising ethno-national partisan' but 'the national conflict has been the primary source of antagonism, violence and constitutional stalemate'.[15]

Marxist accounts

Since the outbreak of 'the Troubles' there have been a number of additional competing explanations for the nature and intractability of the conflict in Northern Ireland. One such explanation derives from Marxist accounts. In his important evaluation of the literature on the region, *Interpreting Northern Ireland*, John Whyte notes the contribution of Marxist writings to the study of Northern Ireland. He maintains that 'Any fair-minded non-Marxist must agree that the study of Northern Ireland would be the poorer if no Marxist had written on it'.[16] These writings ultimately seek to develop a class analysis of the conflict in the interests of the working class. The traditional Marxist view in Ireland argued that the root of the problem lies in British imperialist involvement in Ireland and that Britain must withdraw from Northern Ireland for the realisation of a socialist united Ireland. Following British withdrawal Catholics and Protestants would then unite in class solidarity and the conflict would come to an end.

McGarry and O'Leary introduce the position of 'Green Marxism' whereby British imperialism and capitalism are seen to be the primary causes of the conflict.[17] The vein of this argument goes back to the writings of James Connolly leading up to the 1916 Easter Rising who claimed that the 'cause of labour is the cause of Ireland' and tied socialist objectives with the struggle for national independence. This Marxist interpretation looks back to the time of the Plantation by English and Scots settlers and argues that Ireland was exploited by landlords who aggravated tensions between Catholics and Protestants. Socialism and an end to sectarianism will, therefore, only come about with an end to partition.

McGarry and O'Leary point out that the claim of Green Marxists that a socialist Irish state would bring about an end to sectarian divisions does not account for the wishes of the Protestant community to remain within the United Kingdom. As evidenced by their commitment to the Union, it is hardly likely that the force of their British national identity would revert to an attachment to a united Ireland following a socialist revolution. Due to the depth of their commitment to Britain, the British Government is then unlikely to withdraw against the wish of the majority in Northern Ireland to remain within the UK.

The alternative Marxist perspective looks to the uneven economic development between the traditionally more industrialised north and the more agrarian south as an explanation of the conflict. This argument claims that the conflict is, therefore, not about British imperialism and they point to the Protestant support for the Union as evidence that there is no desire for working-class Protestants to be subsumed into a socialist united Ireland. This position suggests that the main divisions in Northern Ireland are along class lines rather than national, ethnic, religious cleavages which are much less important. They suggest that an end to discrimination and the removal of inequalities will bring about class solidarity between the Catholic and Protestant working class. The difficulty with this position, however, lies in the unlikelihood that many nationalists will abandon their aspiration for a united Ireland.

It is important to note that the Marxist accounts are no longer a dominant theoretical perspective on the Northern Ireland conflict. Whyte notes that Marxist writers fail 'to agree on their conclusions' and 'on the nature of the British presence, or the best future for Northern Ireland'.[18] McGarry and O'Leary point to the collapse of Marxism in the 'wider world of ideas' and describe the perspective as another 'broken image' of the conflict in Northern Ireland.[19] The appreciation and critique of such perspectives, however, can help focus our understanding of the nature of the divisions between the two communities. The ethno-national nature of the conflict is a much more appropriate explanation as ethno-national identity is much stronger than class identity. As McGarry and O'Leary note: 'There is little evidence from Northern Ireland, or from other deeply divided ethno-nationally mixed territories, that transcendent class-consciousness can be easily or successfully promoted as an alternative to nationalist mobilization'.[20] The conflict is, therefore, not a consequence of capitalism that will disappear in a socialist state, either a socialist united Ireland or a reformed Northern Ireland.

The colonial interpretation

Another interpretation, held by republicans, maintains that the conflict was a consequence of the colonisation of Ireland by Britain. As Tonge puts it, for republicans 'The "war in the North" against

British rule, episodic after partition but sustained from 1970 until the mid-1990s, was justified as "unfinished business" – a struggle for national liberation against a foreign occupying force'.[21] Thus, republicans believed that the Irish Republican Army (IRA) armed campaign was a necessary reaction to the presence of colonial forces; violence would ultimately lead to British withdrawal from Ireland. This interpretation claims that partition was imposed by Britain against the wishes of the majority of Irish people. The continued involvement of Britain, therefore, denies the realisation of the legitimate aspiration of a united Ireland. To illustrate their contention of the conflict, republicans point to what they see as colonialist-type behaviour of the British state: the introduction of internment; extensive security powers; and the removal of trial by jury.

There are, however, important problems with the colonial interpretation of the conflict. Most importantly, it ignores the existence of the unionist community and its desire for Northern Ireland to remain within the UK. Moreover, colonial arguments fail to recognise that unionists choose to identify as British. The traditional republican position held that unionists were really Irish and that they would acknowledge their 'Irishness' following British withdrawal. More recently, this denial of unionists by republicans has changed to a need to persuade them of the merits of Irish unity. As Tonge notes, Sinn Féin's *Towards a Lasting Peace in Ireland*, published in 1992, included more of an acceptance of the presence of the unionist community.[22] The colonial argument thus also failed to appreciate that British sovereignty continued in Northern Ireland due to the wish of a majority of people there. Indeed, the British Government has pledged to retain the link so long as a majority wishes it and to legislate otherwise should a majority support a united Ireland in the future.

Consociational theory

The theoretical perspectives advanced to explain the conflict lead us to consider the theoretical debates on how the conflict should be resolved. Indeed, a number of theoretical approaches relate to how such ethnic conflicts might be resolved and how democratic institutions in post-conflict states might be designed. A great deal of the literature on conflict resolution is concerned with how to deal with the competing aspirations of the antagonistic communities in a multi-ethnic state, particularly in relation to self-determination issues and power sharing.

Consociationalism is the primary theory advanced as a way to manage ethnic conflict. The theory focuses on how to bring about democracy in divided societies *via* power-sharing institutions. Consociationalism was developed by Dutch political scientist Arendt Lijphart in the 1970s who promoted the approach as a model for introducing and developing democracy in divided societies. In his major work, *Democracy in Plural Societies*, Lijphart suggests:

> it may be difficult, but it is not at all impossible to achieve and maintain democratic government in a plural society. In a consociational democracy the centrifugal tendencies inherent in a plural society are counteracted by the cooperative attitudes and behaviour of the leaders of the different segments of the population.[23]

Lijphart suggests that four key ingredients are needed for consociational democracy to be established: a grand coalition; proportionality; mutual veto; and segmental autonomy. The most important element is the grand coalition whereby all of the main segments in society are represented in government, thus allowing for the politicians representing the opposing ethnic groups to cooperate and compromise. The proportionality principle stipulates that all significant segments should have proportional weight in decision making, while the mutual veto offers political protection for minorities to prevent decisions being made which are against their vital interests and segmental autonomy ensures that a community can make its own decisions in important cultural matters.

Lijphart's theory has been subject to intense scholarly debate since the 1970s, with a number of political scientists providing an important critique of the consociational approach. Much of the debate focuses on whether the consociational approach may actually entrench ethnic divisions rather than promoting accommodation towards a resolution of the conflict. For instance, Rick Wilford writes that consociationalism 'conveys a rather bleak view of humanity' in the sense that it maintains and cements segregation rather than breaking down the boundaries in ethnic conflict.[24] Instead, 'integrationists' propose that ethnic identity is more fluid than consociationalists assume and focus should, therefore, be given to integration between the two communities and cultural diversity.

This alternative perspective to consociationalism is termed the **integrative approach to power sharing** which recommends a greater focus on transcending the nationalist/unionist dichotomy by promoting integration between the two communities. The position advocates increased integration in housing and education and a political system which will promote grass-roots integration and incentives for political parties to cooperate with their ethnic opponents. The 'social transformation' approach is suggested by Rupert Taylor who proposes that ethnic conflict should be transformed, not regulated, as appears with consociationalism. Instead, he argues:

> a social transformation approach, which is concerned to transform the conflict by promoting participatory democracy and challenging ethno-nationalism, holds the promise for peaceful change. It is maintained that attention must turn to the actions of inclusive pro-democracy movements in society which seek to create new relationships of social interaction that transcend divisive boundaries.[25]

The alternative approaches to consociational democracy suggest a focus on more 'integrative' solutions to institutional design in divided societies. In contrast to Lijphart's approach, Donald L. Horowitz offers a critique of consociationalism and suggests that the political system should contain incentives for political elites to accommodate and behave moderately. He argues that the electoral system should promote vote pooling by parties across the ethnic divide. For instance, in multi-ethnic constituencies with a number of political parties contesting elections, the idea is to encourage parties to seek second or third preferences from voters in other ethnic groups, thereby promoting cooperation and encouraging parties to adopt a more moderate position. As Horowitz writes:

> Where the incentive approach is pursued, political parties and leaders who pursue conciliation are rewarded. The main mechanism is an electoral system that induces political parties to rely for their margin of victory on the votes of members of groups other than their own . . . Parties are still ethnically based; but, if the incentives to seek votes across group lines are strong enough, multi-ethnic coalitions of moderate parties of the respective groups may form to exchange the votes of their supporters in various constituencies.[26]

It would appear that there are risks involved for parties pursuing a more moderate approach in a divided society. In pursuing inter-ethnic cooperation and moderation a political party in an ethnic system such as Northern Ireland would be open to accusations of being 'soft' on central issues and of 'selling out' to the 'other side'. However, Horowitz adds that the 'compromising middle coalition then acts to fend off the uncompromising parties on its flanks'.[27] The integrative approach also critiques the consociational principle of a grand coalition in a divided society whereby all of the main segments in society are represented in a power-sharing government. Integrationists believe that this leaves an inadequate opposition in parliament and that it would be better for a smaller number of parties to come together to form a government with a willingness to compromise.

In response to these criticisms, McGarry and O'Leary suggest that the inclusion of radical parties in a grand coalition-type arrangement can make them less extreme whereas exclusion of such parties can destabilise power-sharing institutions.[28] In response to the critique that consociationalism entrenches ethnic divisions they argue that the theory has important long-term potential: 'Consociational democracy . . . is based on the accommodation of rival communities . . . an extended period of voluntary inter-group cooperation should reduce inter-community divisions rather than maintain or deepen them'.[29] Power-sharing theory will be considered throughout the book, particularly in relation to the institutional framework of the Good Friday/Belfast Agreement of 1998 and the post-suspension proposals for the restoration of devolved government.

• •

What you should have learnt from reading this chapter

There are a number of theoretical perspectives in the academic literature advanced to explain the conflict in Northern Ireland:

- The dominant and most appropriate explanation shows that the conflict should be understood as ethno-national rather than simply religious.

- The root of the problem lies in the opposing national identities of nationalism and unionism with the two communities stressing their competing claims to self-determination.

- There is an intense and ongoing theoretical debate on how conflict in divided societies should be resolved. This debate focuses on the consociational and integrative approaches to power sharing.

Glossary of key terms

Consociationalism A theory of power sharing in divided societies which advocates four elements for promoting democratic stability: grand coalition; proportionality; minority veto; and segmental autonomy.
Ethnicity Group identification based on a common descent, culture, language and religion which serve as the demarcations of a given community.
Ethno-nationalism The ethnic group strives for political autonomy and unity on the basis of their identity as a 'nation'.
Integrative approaches to power sharing Alternative approach to consociational democracy which promotes the integration of the different groups in a divided society and incentives for political parties to behave moderately.

Likely examination questions

Explain and discuss the nature of the conflict in Northern Ireland.

Is the Northern Ireland conflict simply based on religious differences?

Helpful websites

The Northern Ireland Life and Times Survey: http://www.arc.ac.uk/nilt

Conflict Archive on the Internet: http://cain.ulst.ac.uk

Suggestions for further reading

John McGarry and Brendan O'Leary, *Explaining Northern Ireland: Broken Images*, Oxford: Blackwell Publishing, 1995.

Brendan O'Leary and John McGarry, *The Politics of Antagonism: Understanding Northern Ireland*, London: Athlone Press, 1993.

Jonathan Tonge, *Northern Ireland*, Cambridge: Polity Press, 2006.

John Whyte, *Interpreting Northern Ireland*, Oxford: Clarendon Press, 1990.

CHAPTER 2

Background to the Conflict

Contents

Overview

The chapter begins with a summary of the historical background to the conflict leading up to partition in 1921 and the creation of Northern Ireland. It then provides an overview of the Stormont administration and why it fell. Attention is given to the objectives of the civil rights movement in pressing for equality for Catholics in housing, employment and voting rights. The return to direct rule and the onset of 'the Troubles' is explored, looking at the re-emergence of the IRA and the arrival of British troops. The chapter also highlights the communal divisions in Northern Ireland in relation to education, culture, sports and residential segregation.

Key issues to be covered in this chapter

- The roots of the conflict and the creation of Northern Ireland
- The Stormont administration: 50 years of unionist control
- How the civil rights movement and the inter-communal violence led to the collapse of Stormont and the onset of 'the Troubles'
- How the two communities are divided in relation to education, sports and culture

The historical context

As in other divided societies throughout the world, history is a particularly contentious topic in Northern Ireland. Contention often derives from the different, and frequently conflicting, interpretations of the history of the conflict by its protagonists. This is certainly the case in Northern Ireland as the nationalist and unionist communities refer to past events to help explain the legacy of their grievances. Historical narrative, myth, collective memory and symbols linked with the past are part and parcel of the conflict. There is even some debate between the two communities as to whose ancestors settled first on the territory that is now Northern Ireland. While nationalists trace their lineage back to the Gaels who arrived in Ireland in the fifth century, some unionists claim that Scottish tribes, the Cruithin, settled in Ulster before the arrival of the Gaels.

The roots of the conflict in Northern Ireland can be traced back to the Anglo-Norman invasion of 1169. The conquest of Ireland by English monarchs in the sixteenth century led to the Plantation of Ulster in the seventeenth century. The Plantation involved colonisation and the native Gaelic Irish were dispossessed of their land which was given to the Scots and English settlers. Further conquests took place under Oliver Cromwell in the seventeenth century (1649–52). The Cromwell Plantation involved the transfer of nearly all land from Catholics to Protestants. As a result of the Plantations Ireland was populated by different groups who were divided by language, religion and status. For instance, the Gaelic Irish were Roman Catholic, while the Scots settlers were Presbyterians and the Anglo-Irish were mostly Anglican/Church of Ireland.

In 1685 James II became king but was soon replaced in 1688 as the 'Glorious Revolution' saw the Dutch Prince William of Orange and his wife Mary, daughter of James II, jointly offered the English Crown by parliament. Catholic Ireland, however, remained loyal to King James and on 12 July 1690 William defeated James' forces at the Battle of the Boyne, which is commemorated on that date each year by unionist parades in Northern Ireland. Further land confiscation from the Catholic Irish to the settlers followed William's victory at the Boyne. William's victory was also followed by the introduction of a series of repressive 'penal laws' which were implemented from 1690 to the

1720s. Under these laws Catholics were excluded from the political establishment and were subject to harsh social measures: they had no representation in parliament; they were banned from owning property; banned from membership of the army, legal profession, public office or becoming MPs; Catholic schools and burials were made illegal; and inter-marriage with Catholics was banned. These laws had a considerable impact on the Catholic population. As O'Leary and McGarry note, 'By the time of the Relief Act of 1778, under which Catholics could acquire leases of land for indefinite tenure if they took the oath of allegiance, Catholic ownership was reduced to 5 per cent of all land in Ireland.'[1] By the late eighteenth century these was some repeal of the penal laws such as the 1793 Catholic Relief Act which gave Catholics the right to vote for MPs. However, this was on a restricted property franchise and Catholics still did not have the right to sit in parliament.

In response to the harsh practices and the cementing of English rule in Ireland the Irish Presbyterian Wolfe Tone formed a group named the United Irishmen in 1791 which aimed to establish Ireland's independence from England. They planned a rebellion in 1796 but the exercise failed as the supporting French invasion fleet was unable to land at Bantry Bay due to storms. Rebellion again broke out in 1798 but was defeated at the Battle of Vinegar. This revolutionary movement was soon replicated in the formation of other organisations such as Young Ireland and the Irish Republican Brotherhood (IRB). The 1798 rebellion was later followed by small rebellions in 1803, 1848 and 1867. These campaigns were designed to destroy the link between Ireland and Great Britain under the 1801 Act of Union. Under the Act the Irish parliament was formally integrated into the parliament of Great Britain and Ireland.

In the 1820s and 1830s, Daniel O'Connell led a campaign for Catholic emancipation. The 1829 Catholic Emancipation Act allowed Catholics to stand for the Westminster parliament, but O'Connell continued his campaign, organising public demonstrations for the repeal of the Act of Union and for a Dublin parliament. Just as the Act of Union was opposed by the Catholic nationalists, it was fervently supported by the Protestant community. According to O'Leary and McGarry, 'the Union became the bulwark of the colonial settlers and their descendants: the Anglo-Irish nobility throughout Ireland and the Protestants of Ulster'.[2]

Box 2.1 Major historical events

1169	Anglo-Norman invasion of Ireland
1600s	Conquest under Oliver Cromwell and Plantation
1690	Prince William of Orange defeated King James II at the Battle of the Boyne
1690–1720s	Repressive penal laws against Catholic population
1793	Catholic Relief Act
1798	United Irishmen rebellion
1801	Act of Union
1829	Catholic Emancipation Act
1845–51	Great Famine

The pursuit of constitutional reform was tempered by the Great Famine, caused by the failure of the potato harvest (1845–51). Over one million people died due to the famine and within four years over one million people were forced to emigrate. The famine was also to have an effect on Anglo-Irish relations as food continued to be exported despite the hunger of the local population, thereby feeding the perception that England failed to stop the starvation and aggravated an already desperate situation. The impact of the famine was less significant in Ulster due to the growth of engineering which developed into a strong shipbuilding industry by the end of the nineteenth century.

Home Rule and partition

A crucial period in the history of Northern Ireland concerns the **Home Rule** debate and the eventual partition of Ireland in 1920. By the end of the nineteenth century a constitutional movement for Irish self-government had developed. The campaign for Home Rule gathered momentum under the leadership of Charles Stewart Parnell, leader of the Irish Parliamentary Party. The campaign was resisted by successive British governments and the settler population. However, as the Irish Parliamentary Party held the balance of power at Westminster following the 1885 election, Parnell persuaded Gladstone to support Home Rule for Ireland in return for his party's support for the Liberal government. Gladstone's stance was, however, bitterly opposed by the Conservatives and the Protestant population in Ulster. Gladstone's party split over the issue and a faction of Liberal Unionists helped defeat the first Home Rule Bill (1886) by 343 votes to 313.

In 1892 the Irish Parliamentary Party once again held the balance of power at Westminster and a second Home Rule Bill was introduced by Gladstone in 1893. The bill was passed by the Commons but was immediately overturned by the House of Lords. The Liberals lost their overall majority in the two elections of 1910, but Asquith formed a new government in January 1911 and his cabinet began to draft the third Home Rule Bill.

There was considerable resistance to the Home Rule movement from unionists. In 1905 the Ulster Unionist Council (UUC) was set up with the aim to resist Home Rule. In response to the developments at Westminster and the drafting of the Home Rule Bills, the UUC announced in September 1911 that it was preparing to establish a provisional government in Ulster. The anti-Home Rule campaign was led by Edward Carson, leader of the Irish Unionist Party. For unionists, Home Rule was unacceptable as it could potentially lead to the development of a Catholic Irish republic which would threaten their British identity. In January 1912, in response to these fears, the Ulster unionists trained a militia of thousands of Protestants which became the Ulster Volunteer Force (UVF).

The third Home Rule Bill was introduced a few months later in April 1912 and proposed an all-Ireland parliament, although supreme sovereignty would be retained at Westminster. In September 1912 the Ulster Unionist Council published 'Ulster's Solemn League and Covenant' and demanded that Ulster be excluded from the Home Rule Bill. The Bill was rejected by the Lords in January 1913 and vetoed again in July. In September 1913 the UUC turned itself into a provisional government ready to take over the administration of the province after the passage of the Home Rule Bill. In June 1914 the government's amending bill to permit temporary exclusion by county was introduced in the Lords, which then altered the amending bill and provided for the exclusion of all of Ulster. On 12 July 1914 the UUC declared itself the provisional government of Ulster. The onset of the First World War then prevented the immediate resolution of the Home Rule crisis. The Home Rule Bill was passed into law in September but was made subject to a new suspensory act which delayed its operation until after the war.

The postponement of Home Rule due to the war and the resistance of the Ulster unionists prompted the IRB to organise an insurrection which became known as the Easter Rising of 1916. The Rising was led by members of the IRB by names which have become synonymous with Irish republicanism: Connolly, MacDonagh, Pearse and Plunkett. The IRB set up its headquarters in the General Post Office in Dublin and issued the Proclamation of Poblacht na hÉireann (Irish Republic). English troops were deployed in Dublin following the surrender of the rebels after five days. Although the Rising failed militarily, the execution of sixteen of its leaders led to growing public sympathy with their goal of Irish independence.

The increased support for the goals of the Easter Rising was then garnered by the republican party Sinn Féin which merged with the IRB in 1917. At the December 1918 Westminster election Sinn Féin won twenty-five unopposed seats and a total of seventy-three of Ireland's 105 seats. However, the new Sinn Féin MPs adopted an abstentionist position and refused to take their seats at Westminster. Instead, they convened at 'Dail Éireann', the Irish parliament, from January 1919. With Sinn Féin not attending the House of Commons, the details of Home Rule were left to the Ulster unionists. The victory of Sinn Féin impacted on unionists' attitudes and led to their support for a separate northern state. Furthermore, the unionists had important bargaining power in the Commons due to their dominant position along with the Conservatives in the coalition headed by Lloyd George.

In 1919 the fourth Home Rule Bill was drafted and became the Government of Ireland Act 1920. The Act became law on 23 December 1920 and created two jurisdictions in Ireland, each with its own Home Rule parliament, one in Belfast and one in Dublin. The parliament in Northern Ireland was bi-cameral with a fifty-two-member House of Commons and a Senate of twenty-six members. Northern Ireland was also still to be represented at Westminster by thirteen MPs. The Act also provided for a Council of Ireland to facilitate the reunification of Ireland subject to the consent of both Irish parliaments.

The Ulster unionists were prepared to accept Home Rule subject to partition. This condition meant that at least six or nine counties

Box 2.2 Home Rule timeline

1886	First Home Rule Bill
1893	Second Home Rule Bill
1905	UUC was formed
1911	UUC announced intention to form a provisional government in Ulster
1912	Ulster unionists trained militia which became the UVF
1912 (April)	Third Home Rule Bill
1912 (September)	UUC published 'Ulster's Solemn League and Covenant'
1914	Government's bill amended in the House of Lords to exclude all of Ulster; delayed due to First World War
1916	Easter Rising
1919	Fourth Home Rule Bill
1920	Government of Ireland Act 1920 became law; created two jurisdictions and two parliaments, Dublin and Belfast
1919–21	War of Independence between the IRA/IRB and Britain
1921	Anglo-Irish Treaty; independence for twenty-six counties of the Irish Free State

would remain outside the jurisdiction of an Irish parliament. As O'Leary and McGarry comment: 'Home Rule in Northern Ireland would provide Unionists with an effective bulwark against the untrustworthy intentions of London governments and the claims of Irish republicans'.[3] On the basis of the Protestant: Catholic ratio in Ulster, unionists lobbied to ensure that the new jurisdiction would control the six counties of the east rather than the nine of historic Ulster. Partition thus guaranteed a clear Protestant/unionist majority. The details of partition were to become an important source of contention and antagonism. It set the scene for an inequitable situation: the Catholic/nationalist population was over a third of the population of Northern Ireland and they were the majority in the counties of Fermanagh and Tyrone and the city of Derry/Londonderry.

Importantly, unionist support for a six-county state grew against the backdrop of the 1919–21 War of Independence where IRB/IRA volunteers fought against the forces of the Crown and the British state. In December 1921 the Anglo-Irish Treaty was signed by the British Government and Sinn Féin. Under the Treaty, Britain provided for Irish independence for the twenty-six counties as the Irish Free State. This granted Ireland dominion status within the British Empire and required Ireland's allegiance to the British king. The Treaty then led to a split in Sinn Féin and ultimately the Irish Civil War fought between pro- and anti-Treaty forces on the issues of whether it afforded an opportunity for full independence and Ireland's position within the British Commonwealth. Northern Ireland remained within the United Kingdom. The Treaty also provided for a Boundary Commission to determine the boundaries between Northern Ireland and the rest of Ireland.

The Stormont regime

With the birth of the Northern Ireland state, the Protestant majority remained unionist while the Catholic minority was hopeful for the eventual reunification of Ireland. The dominance of the Ulster Unionist Party (UUP) via electoral reform, the redistribution of electoral districts and a system of discrimination against the minority led to the installation of an ethnic regime which lasted from 1921 until the fall of the Stormont government in 1972.

The devolved Northern Ireland government within the UK had complete autonomy over law and order and considerable independence in domestic public policy. It remained dependent upon the British Treasury, however, and control of foreign policy was retained by London. Northern Ireland's first Prime Minister was James Craig, a former leader of the anti-Home Rule movement with Edward Carson. Craig was Prime Minister of Northern Ireland from 1921 until his death in 1940. In the Northern Ireland general election of May 1921, all forty unionist candidates secured seats whereas the Irish Party and Sinn Féin got six seats each. Indeed, the UUP would win all elections for the Northern Ireland parliament between 1920 and 1969.

Despite the truce that led to the Anglo-Irish Treaty, violence continued in Northern Ireland. To discuss the situation a meeting took place in 1922 between James Craig, Prime Minister of Northern

Ireland and Michael Collins, Chairman of the Provisional Government of the Irish Free State. In what became known as the 'Craig/Collins pact', the two men agreed that the Boundary Commission on Northern Ireland's borders would have representatives from both jurisdictions and that they would mutually agree on the final details of the border. The pact failed, however, largely due to mistrust between the two sides as well as the issue of expelled Catholic shipyard workers.

As provided for in the Treaty, the Boundary Commission undertook its investigations into the drawing of the Northern Ireland border in 1925. In the end, the Commission was to secure Northern Ireland's boundaries as set out in the Government of Ireland Act. An agreement to this effect was reached between the British, Irish and Northern Ireland Governments. The governments also agreed that there would be regular contacts north and south. These did not take place, however, and the prime ministers of Northern Ireland and the south did not meet until Terence O'Neill and Sean Lemass met in 1965.

Discrimination against the minority

The academic literature on Northern Ireland provides detailed analysis of the system of discrimination against Catholics which existed under the Stormont regime. At an important level, this discrimination was evident in comments of the government and the unionist political elite. For instance, Bew, Gibbon and Patterson note that Craig 'moved towards a much more sytematised adoption of anti-Catholic sectarian rhetoric, both on his own part and that of other members of his government'.[4] Indeed, Craig spoke of a 'Protestant parliament and a Protestant state'. In maintaining unionist rule, discrimination was practised against Catholics in the areas of employment, electoral politics and the allocation of public housing.

An important vehicle for maintaining unionist domination of power was the electoral system. The change of electoral system and the **gerrymandering** of local government jurisdictions served to cement unionist control over Catholic nationalists. In 1922 the Government abolished the system of proportional representation and replaced it with the plurality electoral system of first past the post. The outcome was that electoral competition was always going to be unionist versus nationalist. The redistribution of electoral boundaries (**gerrymandering**) secured the dominance of the UUP. For example in Derry/Londonderry, a unionist majority was returned at local elections despite a large Catholic majority population. This was because the electoral boundaries were drawn in such a way as to return a majority of unionists. The party remained in power for fifty years and during that time Northern Ireland had only six prime ministers, two of whom held office in the latter three years: James Craig (1920–40); John Andrews (1940–3); Basil Brooke (1943–63); Terence O'Neill (1963–9); James Chichester-Clark (1969–71); and Brian Faulkner (1971–2).

It is also important to note that the franchise at the local government level was restricted to rate payers and their spouses. The property requirement disproportionately affected Catholics, although poorer Protestants were in the same situation. Catholics were also discriminated against by the business franchise as company directors had up to six votes each. With unionists dominant in local government they were, therefore, able to maintain control over areas such as housing allocation and planning. As housing was largely segregated with the two communities living apart, this maintained electoral outcomes in favour of unionists.

Throughout the Stormont years a crucial objective of the unionist leadership was to maintain the cohesion of the unionist community against opposition. As Bew, Gibbon and Patterson note, 'Craig seems to have developed an exaggerated concern for the need to preserve the unity of the Protestant bloc'.[5] The authors note that this was not always shared by Craig's colleagues, 'Yet Craig's patriarchal Protestant style – emphasising the unity of that community to the exclusion of the minority – was the answer to one key problem: how to win elections for the Northern Ireland parliament'. The need for unionist cohesion was thus to the cost of the minority. This is noted by O'Leary and McGarry: 'Since their power was dependent upon maintaining the cohesion of the unionist bloc, they had no clear incentive to make concessions to the minority and every incentive to help their own supporters'.[6]

Developments in the Irish Free State

To understand the motivations of the Ulster unionists, it is also important to look at the developments in the Irish Free State. A significant factor was the unionist fear of Irish irredentism. Following the 1932 elections the Irish Government was formed by the anti-Treaty party Fianna Fáil led by Eamonn de Valera. As Fianna Fáil hoped to attain a united Irish republic, this election result was a considerable source of anxiety for the Unionist Government in Northern Ireland. Furthermore, in 1937 the Free State adopted a new constitution. Under Article Two, it held that the national territory consisted of the whole island of Ireland and Article Three spoke of the re-integration of the national territory under the jurisdiction of the Irish Government.

The Irish Constitution also afforded a special position in society for the Catholic Church. Catholicism thus determined the country's attitudes and value system. In 1948 the Free State set up the Irish Republic, thereby signalling the end of Ireland's inclusion in the British Commonwealth. As noted by O'Leary and McGarry, 'The less Ireland remained within the symbolic trappings of the British empire and the more its internal policies reflected the cultural values of its Catholic majority, the greater the likelihood was that hegemonic control would be entrenched north of the border'.[7] Of additional concern for unionists were the campaigns of violence carried out by the IRA in 1938–41 and its border campaign 1956–62. From the unionist perspective, the IRA activity justified the special security measures. For instance, under the Civil Authorities (Special Powers) Act of 1922, the government had the right to intern people without trial, issue curfews and arrest people without warrant. The IRA border campaign fizzled out by the early 1960s, largely due to the lack of support from the Catholic community.

The Northern Ireland 'state' was based on fifty years of unionist rule that discriminated against the Catholic minority. The Stormont regime was, therefore, a unionist regime and unionists were above all concerned to maintain control and cohesion. Over the course of this period, however, the Catholic minority felt increasingly alienated and eventually came to seek redress. By the 1960s minority grievances were expressed by an organised civil rights campaign which called for an end to discrimination and the reform of the state.

The civil rights movement

As explored in the previous section, the Catholic minority in Northern Ireland faced discrimination in employment, housing and politics. In response, a number of organisations formed in the 1960s to campaign for civil rights for the Catholic community. The movement was to have an enormous impact on the politics of Northern Ireland. The reforms proposed by the O'Neill Government were perceived as too little too late and by the end of the decade the objective of civil rights was replaced with the more traditional anti-partition rhetoric. As the movement changed focus to state brutality, the late 1960s saw an increase in inter-communal violence and the descent into conflict.

O'Neill's reforms

It is important to note that attempts were made by Prime Minister Terence O'Neill to introduce reforms. As Dixon notes, 'The emergence of O'Neill as Prime Minister of Northern Ireland in 1963 led to a modernization of at least the rhetoric of unionism if not the substance'.[8] Given the Government's concern to maintain unionist domination, it is interesting to explore O'Neill's objectives for reform. It is clear that O'Neill wanted to improve relations with the Republic of Ireland, illustrated by his meeting with the Taoiseach Séan Lemass in 1965. Of course, for O'Neill, increased contact with the south would lead the Irish Government to better understand the unionist position, thereby strengthening the Union.

It can also be said that O'Neill's attempts at reconciliation with the Catholic minority were also to secure Northern Ireland's position within the United Kingdom. In this respect it can be said that O'Neill's reforms were 'pragmatic rather than liberal'.[9] Another factor was O'Neill's concern to win back support from the Protestant working class which had been moving to the Northern Ireland Labour Party (NILP). For instance, in the 1962 Stormont election the NILP won 26 per cent of the vote. Interestingly, the NILP played a role in the background to the civil rights campaign, having advanced issues that would later be taken up by civil rights activists. Although the NILP had support from both Protestants and Catholics, it saw reform as a way of enhancing the legitimacy of the political system at Stormont.

O'Neill's reforms were opposed by unionists as too much and by nationalists as too little. In December 1966 he announced a package of reforms including the abolition of the business vote for Stormont elections and setting up a boundary commission. Importantly, there were a number of constraints on O'Neill which limited the extent of his proposed reforms. For instance, he faced considerable opposition within his cabinet and from unionist backbenchers. Opposition to reform also came from the populist standpoint of Ian Paisley who saw the proposals as a betrayal of unionism. Paisley staged counter-marches to the civil rights demonstration against appeasement to Catholics. The substance of O'Neill's reforms, however, disappointed the Catholic community. The Nationalist Party which became the official opposition at Stormont in 1965 had been unsuccessful in persuading the Unionist Government to introduce adequate anti-discrimination measures. As a result, there was a growth in civil rights organisations with the aim of putting pressure on the Government. In addition to the Campaign for Social Justice which was formed in 1964, the main groups included the Derry Citizens' Action Committee, the Northern Ireland Civil Rights Association and the People's Democracy.

Birth of the civil rights campaign

The civil rights movement was led by a new, expanded Catholic middle class who emerged in the 1960s. This expansion was largely on the back of the British welfare state. Due to the welfare pro-grammes the minority's formal enthusiasm for joining an indepen-dent and united Ireland appeared to take a back seat to the civil rights project. According to O'Leary and McGarry, 'Catholics began to interact more with state institutions and to expect more from them'.[10] It was this interaction with the state that led to the civil rights move-ment. While there was certainly a middle-class element, the move-ment's momentum came from locally-based organisations.[11] With the election of a Labour Government in 1964 the Catholic community had increased expectations that their situation in Northern Ireland would change. They were disappointed, however, thus leading to activism in a different format *via* civil rights street demonstrations.

In January 1967 the Northern Ireland Civil Rights Association (NICRA) was formed and became the umbrella group for the move-ment. The organisation called for universal suffrage at the local government level, anti-discrimination legislation covering public employment and the repeal of the Special Powers Act. It took inspir-ation from the American civil rights demonstrations on behalf of the black population in the Deep South. Austin Currie, a Nationalist MP, had been campaigning on the failure of Catholics to be allocated council housing by unionist-controlled councils. He organised a march from Coalisland to Dungannon in June 1968 to protest against the eviction of a Catholic family. A second march was organised on 5 October 1968 in Derry/Londonderry. Despite the march being banned, marchers went ahead and were attacked by the Royal Ulster Constabulary (RUC), leading to violence between nationalists and the RUC in the Bogside. It was this second march on 5 October that was a turning point for the civil rights campaign.

In October 1968, a small left-wing student group, the People's Democracy (PD) was formed at Queen's University Belfast to campaign for 'one person, one vote' in local elections, fair allocation of housing and the repeal of the Special Powers Act. In November 1968 it appeared that the Unionist Government was responding to these pressures as O'Neill announced reforms including the abolition of the business vote in local elections, impartial allocation of public housing and the review of the Special Powers Act. The PD, however, dismissed the reforms and was intent on transforming the civil rights campaign into a mass movement.[12]

On 4 January 1969 the PD organised a march from Belfast to Derry/Londonderry which was ambushed by loyalists including off-duty members of the Ulster Special Constabulary (the B Specials) at Burntollet Bridge. The loyalist attack inflamed the situation which became increasingly polarised along sectarian lines. The result of Burntollet was thus to alter the ethos of the movement. As Dixon notes, 'The agenda was shifting away from civil rights towards RUC brutality and the need to defend nationalist areas'.[13] In contrast, O'Neill's proposed reforms were increasingly seen by unionists as concessions to the civil rights movement. At the Stormont election in February 1969 the divisions within unionism were stark. Despite receiving sufficient support to carry on, O'Neill resigned and was replaced by his cousin James Chichester-Clark in May.

The civil rights movement which had initially hoped to secure its goals via non-violent tactics was overtaken by street violence and sectarian clashes. As English writes, 'The attempt to pursue equal rights for northern Catholics within a UK framework, rather than stress the need to end partition, was one that failed, strangled by the more traditional issue of the struggle between unionism and nationalism'.[14] The process of reform was to be a gradual one: universal suffrage for local elections was introduced in 1969; a Police Authority was set up in 1970; the Director of Public Prosecutions in 1972; the Northern Ireland Housing Executive was set up in 1971; in 1972 local government was reorganised, reducing the extent of control of local councils; and in 1976 the Fair Employment Act 1976 banned discrimination on the basis of religious background.

Focus of the campaigners

Significantly, there have been divergent interpretations of the intentions of the civil rights campaigners. For some, the objective of the movement was to undermine Stormont and bring about a united Ireland. For others, the primary goal was civil rights first to be followed by pressure for a united Ireland at a future date. For many unionists, however, civil rights was simply a tactic to secure a united Ireland and destabilise Stormont. They pointed to the anti-partitionist rhetoric of the civil rights movement. According to Dixon, 'The simultaneous advocacy of civil rights, "British rights for British citizens", with anti-partitionism and the overwhelmingly Catholic/nationalist membership of the civil rights movement led unsurprisingly to a perception that the two demands were linked'.[15]

There was certainly a significant republican input into the movement as a connection can be made between the 1960s IRA and the origins of the civil rights movement. Many of the ideas for a civil rights campaign emerged from the IRA Wolfe Tone Societies and NICRA was founded as a result of these developments.[16] Furthermore, there was certainly republican involvement within NICRA, with IRA volunteers acting as stewards at the marches. Unionists' fears were also compounded both by the call from the Taoiseach Jack Lynch for a UN peace-keeping force and the alleged involvement of some members of the Fianna Fáil Government in seeking to supply arms to the Provisional IRA north of the border.

As the civil rights movement changed its focus from equal rights to the actions of the RUC and the state, increased tension and violence spread across Northern Ireland. Although internal reforms were introduced gradually, many civil rights campaigners saw these measures as too little too late. By the late 1960s the situation descended into further violence and confrontation with the Unionist Government unable to uphold law and order.

Onset of 'the Troubles'

Due to the deteriorating security situation the British Government deployed troops on the streets of Northern Ireland in August 1969. This was shortly followed by the re-emergence of the IRA. The early 1970s was an horrendous time in Northern Ireland, marked by a number of controversial incidents including Brian Faulkner's decision to introduce internment, Bloody Sunday and increasingly alarming violence. The period of conflict known as '**the Troubles**' lasted from the 1970s throughout the 1980s until the peace process of the 1990s. Over 3,500 people were killed, most of them civilians. Victims on both sides lost their lives in a cycle of sectarian murders.

Sectarian violence escalated throughout the summer of 1969. Much of the violence was perpetrated by loyalists following the creation of the new Ulster Volunteer Force (UVF) in 1966. Loyalist rioting took place in parts of Belfast and Catholic families were burned out of their homes. The situation gave rise to heightened sectarianism in Belfast, echoed in Derry/Londonderry at the Apprentice Boys' parade on 12 July where sectarian clashes broke out between Catholic and Protestant crowds. The incident turned into violence between Catholics and the RUC with the police using tear gas and baton charges in what became known as the Battle of the Bogside. The situation led to direct intervention from Westminster as the Unionist Government requested the deployment of troops who arrived on 14 August. However, despite the presence of the British army on the streets, further sectarian violence and the burning of homes ensued.

The violence against Catholics was a crucial factor in the re-emergence of the IRA following a split in the organisation. Over the summer of 1969 the IRA had not been able to provide Catholics with protection against attack. At the December 1969 IRA Convention the organisation decided to abolish abstentionism, thereby recognising the three governments in London, Dublin and Belfast. A group of leading volunteers opposed this development and broke away to set up the Provisional IRA.[17] They wanted to uphold the republican view of the northern state as illegitimate and to return to the organisation's traditional military role.[18] The IRA hoped to win back Catholic support following the attacks in Belfast and it saw military action as the solution to defending the Catholic community and seeking retaliation.[19]

While peace had been temporarily restored with the arrival of British troops, who were initially largely welcomed by the Catholic community, this changed, however, as the British army increasingly came to be seen as defenders of the state. In response, the IRA began an anti-imperialist campaign against the British army. What began in the 1960s as a concern for civil rights was, therefore, transformed into a focus on the constitutional question and the objective of a united Ireland. The violence of 1969 escalated over the next few years with a growth of paramilitary activity on both sides.

As inter-communal violence and fighting between the IRA and the British army continued, the Unionist Government was unable to maintain control. Chichester-Clark's tenure as Prime Minister lasted less than two years. The measures for reform including the disbandment of the B Specials, the creation of a Ministry of Community Relations and a central housing executive were highly contentious for the unionist community. The Prime Minister faced grave security problems, the lack of policing in Catholic 'no-go' areas and pressure from within his party. His tenure was made more difficult due to the Catholic hatred of the army following the imposition of curfews in areas such as the Falls Road in Belfast, sporadic rioting and IRA activity including the murder of three off-duty Scottish soldiers in March 1971.

Chichester-Clark turned to the Conservative Government (since June 1970) in London for help. He disagreed, however, with Westminster on what should be done, leading to his resignation and replacement by Brian Faulkner. In an atmosphere of rioting, burning of homes and the IRA campaign, Faulkner wanted to regain control of law and order, defeat the IRA and retain unionist unity. The British Government was reluctant to get involved and put pressure on the Unionist Government to introduce further reforms. However, Edward Heath granted Faulkner's request to introduce internment without trial on 9 August 1971; a measure the Northern Ireland Prime Minister wanted to counteract the IRA. It was a fateful decision, however, which led to further violence and increased membership of the IRA. As O'Leary and McGarry comment, internment proved 'a political and military disaster'.[20] It was a propaganda coup for the IRA against the Unionist Government and Britain.

The Catholic community's anger against the introduction of internment was such that a demonstration against the measure was organised in Derry/Londonderry on 30 January 1972. In what became known as 'Bloody Sunday' British paratroopers shot dead thirteen unarmed civilian demonstrators. The tragedy attracted global attention and boosted recruitment for the IRA, who in turn stepped up their bombing campaign. The massacre became a lasting grievance for nationalists throughout 'the Troubles'. Following the events of 'Bloody Sunday', the Unionist Government was unable to regain control,[21] and although Faulkner was unwilling to give up control over security, Heath prorogued Stormont and announced direct rule from 1 April 1972. The Northern Ireland Government was replaced by Secretary of State William Whitelaw and the Northern Ireland Office.

On 21 July 1972 the IRA exploded twenty-one bombs in Belfast city centre. In what became known as 'Bloody Friday' nine people were killed, marking the start of cyclical violence and tit-for-tat murders on both sides. 'The Troubles' continued throughout the 1970s and 1980s until the peace process of the 1990s and the signing of the 1998 Agreement. With more than 3,500 people killed and thousands injured and bereaved, the people of Northern Ireland suffered intimidation, paramilitary beatings and a prolonged sense of fear. Horrific events such as Enniskillen, Graham's, Greysteel and Loughinisland are etched in memories as people hope such human tragedy is a thing of the past.

Communal divisions

To understand the divisions between the two communities it is important to look at the way in which society is organised in Northern Ireland. In Northern Ireland people can often tell what community you come from based on your name, school, where you live and the sports you play. The existence of 'two communities' should not be overestimated as there are divisions within each bloc and many people choose not to identify with Catholic/nationalist or Protestant/unionist labels. However, there is a clear degree of inter-communal separation evident in educational and residential segregation, cultural divisions and sport.

Education

In Northern Ireland the vast majority of pupils attend a school according to their religion. Protestant children attend the state or 'controlled' schools and Catholic children attend schools which are governed by the Catholic Church. There are, of course, instances of Catholic pupils attending schools in the 'controlled' sector and some Protestant children attending Catholic schools. In the main, however, Catholic and Protestant pupils are largely educated apart from one another. As educational provision is a crucial socialisation factor, schooling helps inform children's sense of identity. In controlled schools pupils are instilled with a sense of Britishness. There may be some identification with the British Royal family and pupils play sports such as cricket, rugby and hockey. In contrast, Catholic schools convey a sense of Irish identity. Catholic iconography is on display and religious instruction is a vital part of school life. Pupils play Gaelic football, hurling and camogie and there is a focus on Irish history.

Although children in Northern Ireland are largely educated apart from one another, the integrated education sector provides schooling for all children, irrespective of their religious background. Protestant and Catholic children and children of other faiths or none are educated together. The objective of integrated education is to transcend communal divisions, thereby encouraging children to understand and respect each other's differences. The first integrated school, Lagan College, opened in Belfast in 1981 with twenty-eight pupils. In 2006 there were fifty-eight schools educating almost 18,000 pupils.[22] Despite the interest in and growth of integrated schools, the segregated sector remains dominant. However, there is potential development of the integrated sector in the context of the UK Government's *A Shared Future* document published in March 2005. The plan is to promote good relations between the people of Northern Ireland, promote a culture of tolerance, the elimination of sectarianism and racism and a shared community where people live, work and learn together.[23]

Culture and sport

For the Catholic/nationalist community, there is a close association with Irish cultural traditions including music, literature and the Irish language. Indeed, speakers of the Irish language are almost entirely from this community. They see the Irish language as an important part of their national heritage and an expression of identity which needs to be accorded governmental protection and support. However, the Irish language is often perceived as a controversial topic. Due to its identification with the Irish nation, unionists see it as divisive, foreign and threatening their sense of Britishness. Irish is usually not offered as part of the curriculum in 'controlled' schools. Interestingly, the Good Friday/Belfast Agreement set up a North–South Implementation body to support the Irish language on behalf of nationalists and the Ulster–Scots language on behalf of a section of the unionist community. Two new agencies were set up – Foras na Gaeilge and the Ulster–Scots Agency – to promote the respective languages. Ulster–Scots is a speech once used in the countryside and originates from the arrival of Scots settlers in Ulster in the seventeenth century. It celebrates the 'Ullans' language and Scottish music, song and dance.

An important component of unionist culture for many Protestants is the annual marching season. Each year members of the Orange Order take part in parades throughout Northern Ireland to commemorate key events, particularly the Battle of the Boyne of 1690 which is celebrated on 12 July. For the marchers and supporters who line the route to watch the parades, the objective is to commemorate historical events, celebrate the Protestant faith, demonstrate political unity for diverse Protestant denominations, and assert their cultural identity in opposition to the Catholic Church and the idea of a united Ireland.[24] Along with marches organised by the Royal Black Institution and the Apprentice Boys of Derry the Orange Order is an important cultural expression for many Protestants. However, the parades are controversial as they are seen by many nationalists as antagonistic rituals, designed to provoke resentment. The parades are particularly contentious in relation to the march to Drumcree church in Portadown and the Ormeau Road in Belfast as nationalist residents object to the parades marching through their areas.

Sport in Northern Ireland very clearly illustrates the social divisions between the two communities. The Gaelic Athletic Association (GAA) is almost exclusively nationalist and has a very large membership from among the Catholic nationalist population. GAA clubs exist throughout the towns and rural communities and Gaelic football, hurling and camogie are played in Catholic schools. Until 2000 the GAA's Rule 21 prevented members of the security forces from playing Gaelic sports. Cricket, rugby and hockey are more associated with the unionist community and are regarded by many nationalists as British games. While soccer is a sport which is played by both communities, it can be particularly divisive in Northern Ireland. Soccer teams in Northern Ireland are usually supported by one or other community: Linfield is supported by Protestants while Catholics support Cliftonville. There is a Northern Ireland international team which in principle represents both sides. In practice, though, it appeals more to the unionist community and nationalists are more likely to support the Republic of Ireland soccer team. A more positive development is illustrated by the Government's plans to build a new sports stadium in Northern Ireland as a joint enterprise between the GAA, rugby and soccer.

Residential segregation

An important feature of life in Northern Ireland relates to the fact that many people live in areas populated almost exclusively by their 'own' community. While the west of the province is largely nationalist and the east is predominantly unionist, the two communities are unevenly distributed. There are, of course, many mixed areas where Catholics, Protestants and others live together in peace. Yet, it is also true that in some areas Catholics and Protestants often live apart from one another. Segregation is particularly pronounced in working-class areas where the presence of 'peace walls' are designed to keep the two communities apart.

In such 'interface' areas in Belfast local community tensions sometimes trigger violence, instances of intimidation, attacks on homes and even sectarian murder. Such tensions were much in evidence during the Holy Cross dispute which began in June 2001 over access to a Catholic primary school. On one side local residents claimed they were being intimidated by republicans, while on the other, parents pointed to the prevention of their children from going to school by the normal route. The stand-off led to widespread rioting in Belfast with clashes between residents and security forces. In May 2002 First Minister David Trimble (UUP) and Deputy First Minister Mark

Durkan (SDLP) held separate meetings with the groups to resolve the dispute which was finally settled after both sides agreed to a package of enhanced security and social measures. All too often, however, 'interface' areas can become the site of intimidation, fire bombs and attacks on homes.

· ·

✓ What you should have learnt from reading this chapter

The historical background to the conflict in Northern Ireland reaches back at least several centuries. Key events in the past are employed by unionists and nationalists to explain their political goals, identity and heritage.

- The creation of Northern Ireland was itself born out of violence and conflict following the Home Rule crisis, the Government of Ireland Act 1920 and the Anglo-Irish Treaty 1921.

- The Stormont regime upheld unionist rule for 50 years and discriminated against the Catholic minority.

- The civil rights movement aimed to persuade the Government to address discrimination by introducing reforms. Street demonstrations led to sectarian clashes which turned into fighting between Catholics and the RUC.

- In the context of inter-communal violence 'the Troubles' took over with the arrival of British troops and the re-emergence of the IRA.

- Communal divisions continue to pervade society: while people go to work and university together, there is still segregation in education, culture, sports and residential areas.

🔎 Glossary of key terms

Gerrymandering The manipulation of electoral boundaries which was carried out to ensure a unionist majority.
Home Rule movement The campaign to bring about self-government in Ireland.
'The Troubles' The period of conflict in Northern Ireland from the early 1970s until the peace process of the 1990s and the signing of the 1998 Agreement.

Likely examination questions

Why did the Stormont regime collapse?

Explain the onset of 'the Troubles' in Northern Ireland.

To what extent is Northern Ireland a segregated society?

Suggestions for further reading

Paul Bew, Peter Gibbon and Henry Patterson, *Northern Ireland 1921/2001 Political Forces and Social Classes*, London: Serif, 2002.

Dominic Bryan, *Orange Parades: The Politics of Ritual, Tradition and Control*, London: Pluto Press, 2000.

Paul Dixon, *Northern Ireland: The Politics of War and Peace*, Basingstoke: Palgrave, 2001.

Richard English, *Armed Struggle: The History of the IRA*, Basingstoke: Macmillan, 2003.

Thomas Hennessey, *A History of Northern Ireland 1920–1996*, Dublin: Gill and Macmillan, 1997.

Brendan O'Leary and John McGarry, *The Politics of Antagonism: Understanding Northern Ireland*, London: Athlone Press, 1993.

CHAPTER 3

Political Parties and Paramilitaries in Northern Ireland

Contents

Overview

The chapter provides an overview of the main political parties and paramilitary groups in Northern Ireland. It discusses the main parties within the unionist and nationalist blocs, the cross-community Alliance Party of Northern Ireland and the Progressive Unionist Party. The chapter considers the parties' ideological standpoints and their position on Northern Ireland's constitutional status. It also points to any significant intra-party tensions and the parties' response to the peace process leading to the 1998 Agreement. Finally, the chapter explains the role of republican and loyalist paramilitaries in the conflict and points to issues such as decommissioning and criminality.

Key issues to be covered in this chapter

- Electoral competition within as well as between the unionist and nationalist blocs
- The position of the parties in relation to the peace process and the 1998 Agreement
- The difficulty for a cross-community party to gain considerable support
- The role of republican and loyalist paramilitary groups and the move away from political violence

Ulster Unionist Party

The Ulster Unionist Party (UUP) was formed out of the unionist response to the Home Rule movement in the late nineteenth and early twentieth centuries and the formation of the Ulster Unionist Council in 1905. The UUP governed Northern Ireland from 1921 until 1972 and during this period enjoyed hegemonic control of the new state, as evidenced in gerrymandering, discrimination against the minority community and electoral domination. Indeed, the only real electoral competition to the UUP came from the bi-communal Northern Ireland Labour Party (NILP) in the 1950s which became the official opposition after the 1958 election.

The UUP is committed to maintaining Northern Ireland's position within the United Kingdom. Party members profess liberal values and see their Northern Irish identity and culture in similar terms to the other regions of the UK. Importantly, Ulster Unionism is seen to be complex given the party's formal link with the Orange Order which lasted 100 years. The Orange Order had representation on the Ulster Unionist Council and many members of the party were also members of the Order. On becoming UUP leader in 1995 David Trimble made it clear that he wanted to end the party's link with the Orange Order, but his motion was defeated at the 1995 Annual Conference. The link finally ended in March 2005 when the Grand Lodge severed the ties due to restructuring within the UUP.

Intra-unionist relations

A central facet of Ulster Unionism is that it has suffered from considerable divisions, both within unionism as a whole and within the UUP in particular. For instance, a major spilt took place in the late 1960s when Prime Minister Terence O'Neill tried to introduce reforms. The party was divided along pro- and anti-reform lines with the pro-reform unionists later forming the bi-communal Alliance Party of Northern Ireland in 1970. Against the backdrop of the civil rights movement reforms were rejected by William Craig's Vanguard Unionist Party (which split in 1975 over Craig's proposal for a temporary coalition with the Social Democratic and Labour Party (SDLP)) and the DUP. Divisions came to the fore at the time of the Sunningdale Agreement between those who supported UUP leader Brian Faulkner's support for power sharing with nationalists and the Council of Ireland and those who opposed him. By the late 1970s there was clear competition between the two main unionist parties – the UUP and the DUP. According to Mitchell and Wilford in an 'ethnic dual-party system' 'each unionist party attempted to outdo the other in terms of ethnic intransigence'.[1]

This intra-bloc competition did, however, abate for a time in the aftermath of the signing of the Anglo-Irish Agreement (AIA) between Prime Minister Margaret Thatcher and Taoiseach Garret FitzGerald in 1985. The AIA led to a sense of cohesion and unity between the unionist political parties who joined forces to oppose the deal. Under Article Five of the AIA an inter-governmental conference would provide for the Irish Government to put forward views and proposals for legislation and policy with reference to the minority community. For the UUP and DUP, the involvement of the Irish Republic in the affairs of Northern Ireland threatened the Union. Furthermore, a role for the Irish Republic was clearly a success for the SDLP, who had been pushing for an Irish dimension. As Farrington notes, 'The AIA created a disjuncture between political developments and Unionist interests'.[2] The party felt betrayed by the British Government and felt that the SDLP argument for the involvement of the Irish Republic had taken primacy over unionist concerns. Although the UUP and the DUP agreed to an electoral pact at the 1987 Westminster election, tensions were never far from the surface. The parties were unable to agree on a potential alternative to the AIA and the UUP was clearly the dominant unionist party. As Mitchell and Wilford comment, 'Cooperation between the two main unionist parties gradually reverted to competition and then fierce hostility'.[3]

Interestingly, in the period following the signing of the AIA, there was increased focus within the UUP on the merits of further integration of Northern Ireland into the UK. Farrington describes this period as 'the heyday of integrationism'.[4] Integrationists called for the administration of Northern Ireland to be in line with the rest of the UK. Under such a system legislation at Westminster would apply automatically to Northern Ireland and some administrative devolution would be established for the region. Some party members sought electoral integration whereby the Northern Ireland electorate could join and vote for parties in Britain. The UUP then found itself in a favourable position as the party held the balance of power at Westminster following the 1992 elections. The Major Government was, therefore, more amenable to unionist interests and the UUP in particular. However, unionists were somewhat alarmed and disappointed at the British Government's Downing Street Declaration of December 1993 which stated that Britain has 'no selfish strategic or economic interest' in Northern Ireland.

In the mid- to late-1990s there was considerable change in unionist politics. UUP leader James Molyneaux resigned in August 1995 and was replaced by David Trimble. There was also considerable fragmentation of the unionist vote into a number of parties: the UUP; the DUP; the UKUP; the Progressive Unionist Party (PUP); and the Ulster Democratic Party (UDP). It is clear that unionist parties had some difficulty dealing with the wider political climate in these years. Farrington explains that unionists have had no real sense of ownership of the peace process: 'they had a limited input into the [Downing Street Declaration], no input into the AIA or the Framework Documents and no influence on the process of ending violence'.[5]

Response to the 'peace process'

In response to the unfolding peace process of the 1990s, David Trimble was of the view that the UUP needed to take a greater role in the process to influence the outcome. The party had an important role in the inter-party talks 1996–8 which led to the signing of an agreement on Good Friday, 10 April 1998. Indeed, the Agreement was essentially a deal between the UUP and the SDLP. However, even from the moment of its signing the UUP was clearly divided over the deal with Jeffrey Donaldson MP walking out of negotiations. From David Trimble's pro-Agreement perspective, it achieved long-term unionist objectives in cementing Northern Ireland's place within the UK. He pointed to the Irish Government's reform of Articles 2 and 3 of its Constitution as evidence that the Agreement would be a permanent settlement, would end the conflict and secure Northern Ireland's constitutional position within the UK. In contrast, anti-Agreement Ulster Unionists saw the deal as a major concession to Sinn Féin and the IRA.

Undoubtedly, major problems arose for Trimble's leadership over the issue of IRA decommissioning. This was particularly evident in relation to Sinn Féin ministers in government prior to decommissioning and the extent of north–south cooperation. The UUP wanted to see decommissioning before the executive was formed while Sinn Féin called for power sharing prior to decommissioning. The issue was finally resolved in November 1999 when Trimble agreed to 'jump first' to allow for power sharing on the condition that decommissioning took place by February 2000. In addition to Trimble as First Minister, the party had three additional ministerial seats in the new Northern Ireland Executive Committee. The contentious decision to allow a power-sharing government to form including Sinn Féin before IRA decommissioning led, however, to serious strains within the party. Trimble's leadership was frequently called into question and the DUP became the largest unionist party at the 2003 Assembly elections. The party lost three MLAs to the anti-Agreement DUP in January 2004. Trimble lost his Westminster seat at the general election in May 2005 and resigned as party leader. Under new leader Sir Reg Empey the party continued to support power sharing with nationalists but faced electoral difficulties given the DUP's position as the largest unionist party.

Democratic Unionist Party

The DUP has been one of the two major unionist parties since its formation in October 1971. While the party was in second place to the Ulster Unionist Party for years, it more recently became the largest party in Northern Ireland, having outpolled the UUP at the 2003 Assembly elections. The two main unionist parties have been bitter rivals for the unionist vote apart from the brief period of intra-unionist harmony following the Anglo-Irish Agreement of 1985. In terms of the differences between the two parties, Feargal Cochrane suggests that DUP members 'tend to be younger, more populist and to possess a closer link to fundamentalist Protestantism than their colleagues within the Ulster Unionist Party'.[6]

Politics and religion

It is crucial to appreciate that politics and religion are inextricably linked within the DUP. There is a close relationship between the Free Presbyterian Church and the party with many DUP members and councillors also being Free Presbyterians. The Church was formed as a new denomination in 1951 and Ian Paisley became its leader. Grounded in evangelical Protestantism, the Church's theological position is very different to mainstream Protestantism in its focus on conversion and being 'saved' as one's means to salvation. As Bruce puts its, 'evangelicals insist that only those people whom God has called and who respond to the gospel message will be saved from eternal damnation and hell fire'.[7] Bruce explains that Paisley's political success 'can only be understood if one appreciates the central role which evangelical religion plays in Ulster unionism'.[8] Bruce also explains that Paisley's religious beliefs have been a driving force for the DUP leader: 'He has never disguised the fact that he is a unionist because he is a religiously conservative Protestant'.[9] Moreover, Paisley's recent success must also be down to the fact that he and his party were able to take advantage of the wider unionist community's disquiet at some of the aspects of the 1998 Good Friday Agreement, such as the release of political prisoners and the prospect of Sinn Féin members in government.

According to Feargal Cochrane there are two distinct strands within the DUP: an 'old guard' which is largely rural and adheres to fundamental Protestantism and a 'new guard' who are mainly urban and well educated.[10] For these DUP members, membership of the Free Presbyterian Church is not as evident. While there has been a changing profile of the DUP with increased professionalisation, there is, however, a lack of women in the party. Although Paisley's daughter Rhonda was a councillor in Belfast City Council and Lady Mayoress of Belfast, she launched a sex discrimination case against the DUP in 2006 for failing to secure a post as policy officer in 2004; the case was settled out of court. Two leading female members, Iris Robinson MP MLA and Diane Dodds MLA, are married to senior party members, Peter Robinson and Nigel Dodds, respectively.

The rise of Paisleyism

The rise of Paisleyism first occurred in the 1960s. The DUP was fiercely opposed to the reformist policies of Prime Minister Terence O'Neill. Indeed, it appears that the growth of the Free Presbyterian Church in this period was caused by 'the conflict between O'Neill's reformist Unionism and Paisley's traditionalist stand'.[11] In his opposition to O'Neill, Paisley secured support from both urban working-class loyalists and rural Protestants receptive to his evangelical message. According to Bruce, 'What O'Neillism did for Paisleyism was to raise in a concrete way the possibility of change from being a Protestant society and culture (always threatened by the old enemy within and without) to being a secular modern society in which religious affiliation would be of little consequence'.[12] Paisley accused O'Neill of giving in to the demands of the minority community as rebels set on destroying Northern Ireland. He regarded O'Neill's reformist strategy as one of appeasement and viewed the civil rights campaign as a front for republican rebels. Ultimately, Paisley and the DUP sought to restore majority rule in Northern Ireland and preserve the culture of Northern Ireland as adhering to distinctly conservative Protestant values. Paisley was elected to Stormont in a by-election in 1969 and to Westminster in June of that year for the North Antrim constituency.

In the 1970s the DUP was vehemently opposed to power sharing with nationalists in response to the Sunningdale Agreement which provided for a coalition of Ulster Unionists, the SDLP and the Alliance Party. In opposition to the Sunningdale Executive, Paisley took an active part in the Ulster Workers' Council strike of May 1974 which ultimately put the nail in the coffin of the power-sharing government. Throughout the 1970s the DUP became the main populist loyalist party. In 1979 Paisley was elected as one of Northern Ireland's three MEPs in the first UK election to the European parliament with 29.8 per cent of the vote. This was a position he kept until he stepped down from that role in 2004 and was replaced by party colleague Jim Allister. In the 1980s the party became more secularised, largely due to the approach of Peter Robinson who persuaded the DUP that the party should reach beyond its Free Presbyterian base. These changes allowed the DUP to progress electorally in the 1980s with 23 per cent of the vote at the 1982 Assembly elections and 24.3 per cent at the 1985 local government elections.

Intra-unionist rivalry

While the history of Northern Ireland since the outbreak of 'the Troubles' has seen intense unionist rivalry between the two parties, there was an important period of inter-party harmony in the joint opposition to the Anglo-Irish Agreement of 1985. Given the Agreement's consultative role for the Republic of Ireland in the affairs of Northern Ireland, the two parties were united in their opposition. They were, however, unable to find a political alternative on which they could both agree. While the DUP sought a return to legislative devolution based on majority rule, the UUP was itself divided between those who supported different forms of devolution and those who advocated integration of Northern Ireland into the United Kingdom. The period of inter-party cooperation was short-lived and dissipated in the 1990s given party differences over the direction of the unfolding peace process and the inclusion of Sinn Féin.

Competition between the two unionist parties increased in the lead up to the signing of the 1998 Agreement. While the Trimble camp within the UUP sought to sell the Agreement as a mechanism for cementing the Union, the DUP was of the view that the establishment of cross-border bodies and a North–South Ministerial Council could only mean a slippery slope towards a united Ireland. The DUP therefore campaigned for a 'No' vote leading up to the referendum on the Agreement. In the June 1998 Assembly election it won twenty seats and two ministerial portfolios.

While opposed to the Agreement, the DUP opted to take up its two cabinet posts and adopted a semi-detached position toward the Northern Ireland Executive Committee formed in November 1999. Although the party took up its two ministerial portfolios, Regional Development and Social Development, the DUP ministers did not attend Executive meetings with the other ministers. The party also rotated its ministers from among its members and refused to attend the North–South Ministerial Council. The DUP was able to benefit electorally from the increasing unionist opposition to the Agreement and positioned the party as a more effective custodian of unionist interests than the UUP.

Significantly, the DUP emerged as the largest party in the 2003 Assembly elections with 25.6 per cent of first preference votes and thirty Assembly seats. This total grew to thirty-three seats when three UUP MLAs (Jeffrey Donaldson, Arlene Foster and Norah Beare) joined the party in January 2004. At the 2005 Westminster election the DUP returned nine MPs compared with one Ulster Unionist MP. Interestingly, the DUP appeared to alter its position from wanting to scrap the 1998 Agreement to a position whereby amendments to the deal would be sufficient for devolved power sharing to take place. The more pragmatic members of the DUP leadership were instrumental in leading the party to support the British and Irish Governments' St Andrews Agreement of October 2006. The deal sought to bring the DUP and Sinn Féin together in a power-sharing executive. For the DUP's part, devolution would only be restored on the condition that Sinn Féin supported the Police Service of Northern Ireland, the courts and the rule of law. As Chapter 8 outlines, the DUP reached an agreement with Sinn Féin in March 2007 and entered a power-sharing government with Ian Paisley as First Minister and Martin McGuinness as Deputy First Minister on 8 May 2007.

Social Democratic and Labour Party

The Social Democratic and Labour Party (SDLP) has been the party of constitutional nationalism since its formation in 1970. Born out of the civil rights movement, the party was set up by six Northern Ireland MPs: Ivan Cooper, Austin Currie, Paddy Devlin, Gerry Fitt, John Hume and Paddy O'Hanlon. The party was committed to socialist principles in relation to social and economic issues and sought to unite people from both communities with a focus on reform, civil rights and equality for the minority community. While it aimed for eventual reunification of Ireland the constitutional question was positioned as a secondary concern. For the SDLP, unity would come about on the basis of consent of a majority in north and south, thus acknowledging unionist consent for unity to take place. While unity was a long-term objective, unionists would have to agree to new political structures in an 'agreed Ireland'. The party thus accepted the reality of Northern Ireland and represented the interests of the minority Catholic community.

Power sharing and the 'Irish dimension'

Since the early 1970s the SDLP has focused on the objective of establishing power-sharing government in Northern Ireland as part of an agreed system between unionists and nationalists. The party consistently emphasised what it views as the crucial all-Ireland dimension. The SDLP has been of the view that the Irish Government must play its part in protecting the rights of the minority community and participate in the political process towards a settlement. In 1972 the party published *Towards a New Ireland*, an important document which set out the party's thinking on how to resolve the structure and set up new structures. It called for an interim arrangement on the basis of joint sovereignty between Britain and Ireland. The document remained the core of SDLP policy and informed subsequent position papers and proposals.

Given the party's objective of power sharing and an Irish dimension, the SDLP was positively involved in the Sunningdale Conference on 6–9 December 1973. The talks included the British Government, the Irish Government, the UUP, the SDLP and Alliance. The parties had already agreed for the SDLP, UUP and Alliance to form a power-sharing executive. The SDLP was also keen to establish a Council of Ireland as part of a settlement whereby ministers from the Republic of Ireland and Northern Ireland would take decisions in relation to areas such as agriculture, tourism, health, culture and sport. The Council of Ireland idea was, however, particularly controversial for unionists who believed the institution would afford too much involvement for the Irish Republic in the affairs of Northern Ireland. When the Sunningdale Executive was set up in December 1973, SDLP leader Gerry Fitt became Deputy Chief Executive with senior party members becoming ministers: John Hume as Minister of Commerce; Eddie McGrady as Minister for Executive Planning and Co-Ordination; and Paddy Devlin as Minister of Health.

The Sunningdale Executive collapsed in May 1974 due to unionist difficulties over power sharing, the results of the 1974 General Election and the Ulster Workers' Council strike. Due to the failure of Bill Craig to persuade fellow unionists to set up a voluntary coalition with the SDLP and the failure of the Constitutional Convention in 1976 to respond to minority concerns, the SDLP became increasingly of the view that the British and Irish Governments should take a more proactive role in advancing the political process. The party criticised the British Government's focus on security issues without considering the causes of the conflict and the issue of opposing national identities in Northern Ireland. As Murray notes, 'The SDLP believed that the only way to resolve the Northern Ireland conflict was for the British Government to create the circumstances in which both communities could address the causes rather than the symptoms of the conflict'.[13]

The party wanted the British Government to remove the unionist veto and persuade unionists to negotiate with nationalists and take into account the diverging national identities of the two communities. It continued to call for internal arrangements based on power sharing and an Irish dimension and sought the support of the Irish Government to make these objectives a reality. The party also wanted the British Government to openly support the principles of power sharing and an Irish dimension rather than leaving the responsibility for finding a solution to the local parties. For the SDLP, increased cooperation between the two governments would override what they saw as unionist intransigence. In its *Facing Reality* document of 1977, the SDLP called for the Irish Government to play its part in bringing about new political arrangements in Northern Ireland.

Leadership of John Hume and the New Ireland Forum

To understand the history of the SDLP attention must be paid to the role of John Hume as leader of the party from 1979 until 2001. Hume had important contacts with the Dublin Government and with officials in Westminster, Brussels and the United States. He believed that the core issue of the Northern Ireland conflict was political identity. He defined Irish unity as agreement between the people on the island of Ireland, and sought accommodation of the unionist tradition in a 'New Ireland' and 'unity in diversity'.[14] Hume adopted a post-nationalist political philosophy in the context of greater European integration and increased cross-border cooperation on social and economic matters. He was also to further the party's objective in developing an Anglo-Irish process. According to Murray, by 1979 the SDLP 'believed the only way forward was for the British and Irish Governments to create the necessary political structures within Northern Ireland over and above the heads of the political parties'.[15] The SDLP believed that unionist opposition to progress would be overcome by the British and Irish Governments working together.

The SDLP opposed Secretary of State James Prior's 'rolling devolution' proposals as the plan focused on an internal solution without sufficient regard to the Irish dimension and would curtail Anglo-Irish co-operation. The party believed that a solution to the conflict required new political structures for Northern Ireland and an Irish dimension; the party was not prepared to accept one without the other. At the Prior Assembly elections in October 1982, the party adopted an abstentionist platform where it would contest the election but not take seats. The party then sought an alternative approach to make political progress which became the New Ireland Forum 1983–4 involving constitutional nationalist parties throughout Ireland and led by the Fine Gael Government in Dublin.

The Forum was significant in its recognition of the unionist position. As Murray points out, it 'represented a consensus among constitutional Nationalists for the right of Unionists to be and remain Unionist and stay British'.[16] The New Ireland Forum Report proposed three options: a united Ireland; joint sovereignty of Northern Ireland by the British and Irish Governments; and a federal arrangement. However, it was rejected by the British Government as was made clear with the much-quoted Thatcher response in November 1984 of 'out, out, out' to the three proposed solutions. Despite the negative response of the British, the Report was significant as it set out the principles which led to the Anglo-Irish Agreement in 1985. For the SDLP, the Report helped cement the role of the Irish Government in devising new political arrangements of which an Irish dimension would be a crucial component. The involvement of the Irish Government was subsequently strengthened by the AIA. There was now a designated role for the Irish Government in protecting the rights of the minority community *via* a new Anglo-Irish Secretariat outside Belfast and a commitment to cross-border cooperation. Given the formal recognition of the involvement of the Irish Government in the affairs of Northern Ireland, the SDLP supported the AIA as the basis for arriving at a potential resolution of the conflict.

The SDLP's role in the 'peace process'

It is crucial to appreciate that the SDLP played a major part in persuading republicans to embrace the political process and abandon the 'armed struggle'. In January 1988 initial talks between Hume and Sinn Féin President Gerry Adams were organised by Redemptorist Priest Father Alec Reid. Hume's goal in the dialogue with Sinn Féin was to put pressure on the IRA to cease its campaign of violence. Certainly, the two parties viewed the political situation in different terms and had divergent proposals for ending the conflict. For instance, Sinn Féin sought immediate British withdrawal while the SDLP did not believe the British should withdraw immediately. While both parties agreed on the principle of Irish national self-determination, the SDLP recognised the right of unionists' national identity as British. As outlined below, the 1988 talks started the process by which Sinn Féin would increasingly become involved in the political process. The dialogue between the two party leaders started up again in 1993 and led to the Hume–Adams statement on Irish self-determination and eventually the IRA ceasefire from August 1994.

From the mid- to late-1990s the SDLP was a driving force in the peace process. Indeed, the structures established by the Good Friday Agreement corresponded to structures the party had advocated over many years. This included a power-sharing administration between the two communities and a crucial Irish dimension in the North–South Ministerial Council. As Murray writes, 'The *Good Friday Agreement* represents everything the SDLP has stood for and worked for since its formation'.[17] The party campaigned for a 'yes' vote in the referendum and was rewarded at the June 1998 Assembly elections with the highest number of first preference votes, 21.97 per cent of the vote and twenty-four seats.

At the formation of the Executive in November 1999 SDLP deputy leader Seamus Mallon became Deputy First Minister and three party colleagues took up ministerial positions. However, the party suffered some electoral losses as Sinn Féin became the largest nationalist party at the 2001 Westminster and local government elections. In the period since the suspension of the devolved institutions in October 2002 the SDLP remained strongly committed to the 1998 Agreement. It supported the St Andrews Agreement and continued to work for inter-communal power sharing, the Irish dimension and increased cross-border cooperation.

Sinn Féin

Sinn Féin ('Ourselves') was formed in Dublin in 1905 by Irish nationalist Arthur Griffith and became a broad political movement which garnered much public support in the aftermath of the 1916 Easter Rising for the attainment of an independent Irish republic. Committed to the end of partition, the modern-day (Provisional) Sinn Féin formed as a result of a split at the party's *ard fheis* (convention) in January 1970 into the Official Sinn Féin and Provisional Sinn Féin which was against an end to **abstentionism**. As Richard English writes:

> The break came over the issue of parliamentary abstentionism, an emblem of alternative republican legitimacy. The states in Ireland were, in traditional republican thinking, illegitimate: Britain had no right to partition Ireland . . . To send representatives to the Belfast, Dublin or London parliaments would be to legitimize the illegitimate. One should try to *abolish* the northern parliament, not campaign for seats there.[18]

Sinn Féin and the IRA

The party is the political wing of the Provisional Irish Republican Army (IRA) which also formed out of a similar split in 1969. English notes the intimate/close relationship between Sinn Féin and the IRA as two parts of the same republican movement: 'Not only had Provisional Sinn Féin been created by the IRA, not only did it share the same republican aims and arguments, but it often had overlapping personnel. IRA members or former IRA members formed a significant part of the Sinn Féin leadership'.[19]

In its campaign against British rule, politics took second place to the 'armed struggle' for Sinn Féin. As Murray and Tonge write, 'Given that they had been formed as part of a critique of the over-politicisation of the Republican movement, it was inevitable that the Provisionals appeared to favour militarism over political education'.[20] Due to the decision to boycott the Stormont Assembly, Dáil Éireann and Westminster, there was no real engagement in local politics in the 1970s and Sinn Féin took a lesser role to that of the IRA. However, the status of Sinn Féin grew in the 1980s as a result of political opportunities afforded by the hunger strikes and the party increasingly tapped into the grievances felt by working-class nationalists in Northern Ireland.

Political mobilisation of the republican movement arose from the situation surrounding the hunger strikes in the Maze Prison (Long Kesh to republicans) in October 1980 and again from March 1981. Bobby Sands, a hunger striker and leader of the IRA in the prison, contested and won a Westminster seat in the Fermanagh and South Tyrone by-election in 1981 (Sands and nine fellow hunger strikers later died in prison). The new involvement in politics was part of the party's 'armalite and ballot box' strategy which combined the 'armed struggle' with electoral politics. In the 1982 Northern Ireland Assembly election Sinn Féin won 10 per cent of the vote. Gerry Adams became Sinn Féin President at the 1983 *ard fheis* where he reaffirmed the republican movement's twin strategy of violence and politics, referring to the armed struggle as a 'necessary and morally correct form of resistance in the six counties'.[21] At the 1983 Westminster election Sinn Féin won 13.4 per cent of the vote and Gerry Adams defeated the SDLP's Gerry Fitt to become MP for West Belfast. At the 1986 *ard fheis* there was a motion to end the policy of boycotting the Irish parliament, Dáil Éireann, as some leading republicans viewed the abstentionist policy in the south as a political obstacle. The party voted to end parliamentary abstentionism and agreed to take seats in the Dáil, although the party suffered another split over the issue as some members left to create Republican Sinn Féin.

Towards electoral politics
The late 1980s were marked by overtures towards an increasingly political focus which would later help bring about the peace process of the 1990s. In 1988 discussions commenced between Sinn Féin and the SDLP as the latter's leader, John Hume, sought to persuade republicans to abandon the use of violence to achieve the goal of a united Ireland. In what became the 'Hume–Adams process', there was some initial agreement between the two parties with regard to the right of the Irish people to self-determination. Although the discussions between the two parties did not come to much in 1988, they were highly significant in demonstrating Sinn Féin's willingness to engage in a political process. As English notes, the involvement of Sinn Féin 'indicated an awareness on their part, first, that they themselves had not been able (force or not) to achieve their goal of Irish unity and, second, that some form of broader nationalist alliance or liaison appealed to them'.[22]

The dialogue between Hume and Adams started up again in 1993 and led to the Hume–Adams statement which 'firmly endorsed the crucial nationalist view that the Irish people as a whole possessed the right to national self-determination'.[23] The British and Irish Governments then issued their position in the Downing Street Declaration of 1993 announced by British Prime Minister John

Major and Irish Taoiseach Albert Reynolds. The document supported Irish self-determination on the basis of majority support in Northern Ireland, thereby upholding the consent principle to reassure unionists. Although republicans were disappointed with the two governments' position, the door remained open to further developments. In 1994 the IRA announced a ceasefire and Sinn Féin gradually became involved in the peace process. At the 1996 Forum elections the party polled 15.5 per cent of the vote and seventeen seats. However, at the outset of the inter-party talks Sinn Féin was excluded due to continuing IRA violence resulting from the end of the ceasefire in February 1996 with a bomb at Canary Wharf in London. Following the victory of the British Labour Party at the 1997 general election with Tony Blair becoming prime minister, the IRA renewed its ceasefire in July 1997. This move then allowed Sinn Féin to enter the talks without having to decommission weapons.

Sinn Féin and the Good Friday Agreement

In May 1998 Sinn Féin took the decision to take seats in a Northern Ireland Assembly under the Good Friday Agreement agreed by the parties in April. As Chapter 7 discusses, the Agreement ended direct rule from Westminster and established an Assembly and power-sharing government at Stormont as well as a North–South Ministerial Council, cross-border implementation bodies and a British–Irish Council. Agreeing to a parliament and government in Northern Ireland without securing Irish unity was certainly controversial for many republicans. According to English, 'For republicans to back the deal and to retain their supporters' enthusiasm, it was necessary to present the Good Friday compromise as a step on the road forward rather than as a final destination'.[24] Adams spoke of the deal being a phase of the peace process and 'transitional' towards the goal of Irish unity.

Despite these reassurances from the Sinn Féin leadership, there was important republican opposition to the Good Friday Agreement from Republican Sinn Féin and its military wing, the Continuity IRA and from the 32-County Sovereignty Movement and its military faction, the Real IRA which opposed anything less than Irish unification. For other dissenters from the wider republican movement, the party had agreed to a 'partitionist' settlement and was ready to take ministerial seats in a Stormont government which they had long opposed.

Sinn Féin celebrated the overwhelming 'yes' vote in the referenda on the Agreement. At the Northern Ireland Assembly elections in June 1998 the party polled 17.7 per cent and eighteen seats, which afforded the party two ministerial seats when the Northern Ireland Executive Committee was formed in November 1999. As Henry Patterson notes, the party's electoral successes bore the fruits of the party's involvement in the peace process led by Gerry Adams and Martin McGuinness, 'They had before them the heady vision of being the first transnational party in the European Union with seats in the Dáil, Stormont and Westminster and the possibility of being in government in both Belfast and Dublin'.[25] At the June 2001 Westminster election and local government election, Sinn Féin emerged as the largest nationalist party with 21.7 per cent and 21 per cent of the vote, respectively. Since the 1998 Agreement the party's electoral support has continued to increase its share of Assembly seats (eighteen seats in 1998, twenty-four in 2003 and twenty-eight in 2007). In contrast, the party lost one of its five seats in Dáil Éireann in the Irish Republic's 2007 general election and was ruled out by Fianna Fáil as a potential coalition partner.

In 2002 the Northern Ireland devolved institutions were suspended amid allegations of an IRA spy ring at Stormont and television images of a police raid at Sinn Féin party offices in Stormont were broadcast around the world. The party continued to dominate the nationalist bloc, however, and at the November 2003 Assembly elections the party won 23.5 per cent of the vote and twenty-four seats. Sinn Féin's electoral support continued to grow as evidenced by the 2005 Westminster election when it polled 24.3 per cent of the vote and five seats. Following the St Andrews Agreement in 2006 the party faced a tremendous challenge as it moved towards supporting the police, judiciary and the rule of law in Northern Ireland which it endorsed at a specially convened *ard fheis* in January 2007.

Alliance Party of Northern Ireland

The Alliance Party of Northern Ireland (APNI) was formed in April 1970 by a number of pro-O'Neill liberal unionists who left the UUP.

Alliance has been the main bi-communal, non-sectarian party in Northern Ireland, drawing support from both communities. However, the party has always broadly supported the union of Northern Ireland and Great Britain. While constitutionally unionist, it has been a consistent advocate of power sharing between unionists and nationalists. The Alliance Party participated in the talks that led to the Sunningdale experiment in 1973–4 and had one cabinet member in the Executive, Oliver Napier as Minister of Law Reform. Over the years Alliance has participated in talks with other parties and sought accommodation between the two communities. Significantly, the party has rejected the 'two communities' model of society in Northern Ireland, preferring a 'one community' approach where everyone in Northern Ireland would share a common allegiance.

The Alliance Party has clearly had some difficulty winning votes in Northern Ireland's ethnic party system. As Mitchell and Wilford comment, Alliance 'continues to be squeezed in a party system that remains highly polarised'.[26] This is because of the nature of the 'dual party system' where there is competition *between* as well as *within* the ethnic segments of the society. This competition, therefore, leaves little room for a centre ground, bi-communal party to progress. Indeed, Alliance has never won a Westminster seat. At the 2003 Assembly elections the party's support dropped to 3.7 per cent, although it managed to retain its six seats on transfers from other pro-Agreement parties in the election under proportional representation (Single transferable vote (STV)). The party has performed fairly well at local council level with 5 per cent of the vote and thirty councillors at the 2005 local government elections.

Alliance participated in the inter-party talks that led to the 1998 Agreement and supported the deal as a vehicle for establishing a power-sharing government. It campaigned for a 'yes' vote in the June 1998 referendum and polled 6.5 per cent of the vote and six seats. However, the party was critical of some of the institutional rules under the Good Friday Agreement. It was opposed to the designation of MLAs as 'unionist', 'nationalist' and 'other' in the Northern Ireland Assembly. For Alliance, this system was particularly contentious in relation to key votes in the Assembly which required a majority of unionist and nationalist members without taking into consideration or requiring the support of their MLAs designated as 'other'. On such occasions Alliance members, and ultimately their supporters, had no voice on key votes.

The issue of communal designation of MLAs became more controversial for the party in November 2001 when three Alliance members re-designated from 'other' to 'unionist' to ensure the re-election of David Trimble (UUP) as First Minister with Mark Durkan (SDLP) as Deputy First Minister. Following the suspension of the devolved institutions in 2002 Alliance proposed a number of amendments to the political structures. In January 2004 it launched its 'Agenda for Democracy' document which advocates alternative arrangements to the 1998 Agreement voting rules which it claimed 'institutionalized sectarianism'. The party fared well at the 2007 Northern Ireland Assembly election winning seven seats, including a seat won by Anna Lo, the first Chinese person to be elected to a European legislature.

Progressive Unionist Party

The Progressive Unionist Party (PUP) was formed in 1979 and has been affiliated with the Ulster Volunteer Force (UVF), a loyalist paramilitary group formed in Belfast in 1966. The PUP is a left-wing socialist party which seeks to represent the concerns and views of the working-class loyalist community and to secure the maintenance of the Union. The party was led by Hugh Smyth, one of the founding members, a Belfast councillor who became Lord Mayor of Belfast in 1994. The party's profile heightened further in the same year, particularly in relation to the announcement of the loyalist ceasefire by the 'Combined Loyalist Military Command'.

The PUP contested the election to the 1996 Forum and won two seats, thus providing a platform to participate in the inter-party talks which led to the signing of the 1998 Agreement. The party supported the 1998 Agreement as a good deal for unionism and campaigned for a 'yes' vote in the referendum. At the 1998 Assembly elections the party polled 2.5 per cent of the vote and won two seats for David Ervine and Billy Hutchinson. Ervine was elected leader of the party in 2002 and was a key figure in transforming loyalism. He had been a member of the UVF and served a five-year prison sentence after being caught driving a car bomb. On his release from prison in 1980 he became involved in politics, advocating some engagement with nationalism and republicanism and to separate politics from religion. Ervine was re-elected as an MLA in November 2003, although party colleague Hutchinson lost his seat.

In 2006 Ervine joined the Ulster Unionist assembly group, a move which was later ruled out of order by the Assembly Speaker. In the post-suspension period and at the St Andrews negotiations in October 2006 the PUP supported the restoration of the devolved institutions, particularly as the UVF was opposed to the British and Irish Governments' 'Plan B' which potentially meant increased north–south cooperation. In January 2007 Ervine died following a heart attack and stroke and was replaced as leader by Dawn Purvis. Ervine's death, however, undoubtedly created a void in loyalist politics as he had been the face and articulate voice for his community since the mid-1990s.

Republican paramilitaries

Paramilitary groups in Northern Ireland have used violence in an effort to achieve their political objectives: a united Ireland on the part of republican paramilitaries; and the defence of the Union by loyalist armed groups. The main republican paramilitary group, the Provisional IRA (PIRA) was founded in December 1969 as the result of the republican split within the IRA. The defining issue of the split was the policy of abstentionism which the IRA Army Council had voted against in October 1969. Moreover, the IRA was accused of not defending Catholic communities against loyalist violence in Belfast in the summer of 1969. The Provisionals thus asserted themselves as the 'defenders' of Catholic areas and adopted military action.

As English notes, 'defence was accompanied within the new IRA thinking by retaliatory violence'.[27] Although the start of 'the Troubles' was multi-faceted due to the feeling of alienation and discrimination on the part of the nationalist community, IRA and loyalist violence also played an important role. For republicans, the struggle was an anti-imperialist one; the IRA viewed Britain as responsible for the conflict and sought national self-determination for the Irish people as a whole. The IRA was responsible for more deaths than any other group during 'the Troubles'. English provides

Table 3.1 Main political parties in Northern Ireland

Party	Leader	Ideology and issues	2003 Northern Ireland Assembly election	2005 Westminster election	2007 Northern Ireland Assembly election
DUP	Revd Ian Paisley	Largest unionist party since 2003; committed to maintaining the Union; relationship between party and Free Presyterian Church; evangelical Protestantism; issue of sharing power with Sinn Féin; agreement with Sinn Féin March 2007	25.6 %; 30 MLAs	33.7%; 9 MPs	30.1%; 36 MLAs
UUP	Sir Reg Empey	Committed to maintaining the Union; serious intra-party divisions over 1998 Agreement	22.7 %; 27 MLAs	17.7 %; 1 MP	14.9%; 18 MLAs
Sinn Féin	Gerry Adams	Largest nationalist party since 2001; committed to Irish unity and British withdrawal; previously supported the IRA's 'armed struggle'	23.5 %; 24 MLAs	24.3 %; 5 MPs	26.2%; 28 MLAs

		Table 3.1 (*cont.*)			
Party	Leader	Ideology and issues	2003 Northern Ireland Assembly election	2005 Westminster election	2007 Northern Ireland Assembly election
SDLP	Mark Durkan	Constitutional nationalist party; seeks Irish unity based on majority support north and south; supports internal power sharing and greater north–south cooperation	17 %; 18 MLAs	17.5 %; 3 MPs	15.2%; 16 MLAs
Alliance	David Ford	Cross-community party; difficulty attracting substantial electoral support; supports power sharing	3.7 %; 6 seats	3.9%; no MPs	5.2%; 7 MLAs

a breakdown of the figures: PIRA was responsible for 1,778 deaths, almost half of the total 3,665 people who lost their lives.[28] Civilians were the largest single category of IRA victims as well as members of the British army, the RUC, UDR, fellow republicans, loyalists and prison service officers.

By the early 1990s it was evident that the 'armed struggle' was not going to achieve the IRA's objective of British withdrawal and a united Ireland. As discussed above, Sinn Féin, the political wing of the IRA engaged in dialogue with the SDLP in 1988 and again in

1993. Following tensions over the meaning of the Downing Street Declaration and a review of republican strategy, the IRA announced 'a complete cessation of military operations' in August 1994. However, the ensuing peace process encountered serious difficulties by the end of 1995 as the British Government and unionists insisted on IRA arms decommissioning in advance of talks with Sinn Féin. The IRA responded by breaking its ceasefire with the Canary Wharf bomb of February 1996. In June 1996 all-party negotiations began and the IRA reinstated the ceasefire in 1997.

IRA decommissioning

In the context of the 1998 Agreement the issue of IRA **decommissioning** was an extremely contentious issue, both for some republicans who were reluctant to give up arms and for unionists who wanted to see the IRA giving up its arsenal before the formation of the Northern Ireland Executive in 1999 including Sinn Féin. The Independent International Commission on Decommissioning (IICD) was set up by the British and Irish Governments to oversee the process of paramilitary weapons being put beyond use. The IRA's first act of decommissioning eventually took place in October 2001, followed by further acts in April 2002, October 2003 and the fourth and final act in September 2005. On the basis of this final act of decommissioning the IICD reported that the IRA had put all of its weapons beyond use, that it was no longer engaged in terrorism and it had stopped orchestrated crime, although some individuals were still involved in crime for personal gain. While the two governments and nationalist parties welcomed this announcement, unionist politicians protested at the lack of photographs or 'transparency' of the decommissioning process.

The IRA's activity has also been scrutinised by the Independent Monitoring Commission (IMC) which was set up by the British and Irish Governments in January 2004 to monitor the activity of paramilitary organisations. In October 2006 the IMC reported that the IRA had committed to a political path, had stood down its volunteers and was no longer engaged in terrorism, training or recruitment. The Report stated that while the IRA was no longer directing organised crime, some individuals were still involved in crime for personal gain.[29]

'Dissident' republicans

There are two main dissident republican armed groups: the Real IRA; and the Continuity IRA. The Continuity IRA is the armed faction of Republican Sinn Féin which split in 1986 over the ending of abstentionism. The organisation opposed the peace process and held the view that the IRA's 1994 ceasefire amounted to surrender to the British Government. The Real IRA was formed in October 1997 following a further split in the IRA with a number of members leaving in opposition to the reinstatement of the ceasefire in July and Sinn Féin's participation in talks at Stormont. The Real IRA was concentrated in the border counties and was responsible for the atrocity at Omagh in August 1998 where twenty-nine people and two unborn babies were killed as a result of a car bomb.

Both organisations have been opposed to Sinn Féin's endorsement of the 1998 Agreement and the abandonment of the 'armed struggle'. The Real IRA's political wing is the 32-County Sovereignty Movement led by Bernadette Sands-McKevitt, sister of hunger striker Bobby Sands, and her partner Michael McKevitt. As English notes, the Real IRA 'aimed to uphold an uncompromising and uncompromised Irish republicanism, and to oppose anything . . . that should fall short of Irish unity and independence'.[30] Certainly, there was an ongoing threat of violence from dissident republicans. In October 2006 the IMC reported that dissident republicans were responsible for attempted bomb attacks, recruitment and criminal activity. In January 2007 Sinn Féin President Gerry Adams attempted to reach out to republican dissidents to persuade them of the viability of his 'peace strategy', particularly in relation to his party's move towards supporting the police.

Loyalist paramilitaries

In the late 1960s there was a re-emergence of Protestant paramilitary groups in Northern Ireland. The Ulster Volunteer Force (UVF), reclaiming the name of a group set up to resist Home Rule in 1912, was formed in 1966. The principal loyalist paramilitary group was the Ulster Defence Association (UDA) which was formed in 1971. For these groups, their professed primary objective was to defend the loyalist community against republican violence. However, loyalist paramilitaries displayed an overt sectarian tendency as ordinary Catholics were often the victims of shootings. Just as the IRA had the capacity to undertake grave atrocities, so too were loyalist paramilitaries capable of some of the worst sectarian violence. For instance, the UVF was responsible for a series of car bombs in Dublin and Monaghan on 17 May 1974 which killed thirty-three people.

Following the IRA ceasefire in 1994, the UVF and UDA responded with their own ceasefire from October which was announced by the 'Combined Loyalist Military Command'. As noted above, the political objectives of the UVF have been represented by the PUP, while the UDA was represented politically by the UDP from the mid-1990s until 2001. The UDP broadly supported the 1998 Agreement but failed to win any seats at the 1998 Assembly elections and the party was dissolved in November 2001.

The UDA withdrew its support for the 1998 Agreement in July 2001 as the organisation felt that republicans had gained too many concessions. However, the UDA was involved in violence, leading then Secretary of State John Reid to declare that its ceasefire was no longer recognised following a police report that claimed the UDA was responsible for rioting and a pipe-bomb campaign against Catholics. In February 2003 the UDA announced a twelve-month period of 'military inactivity' which was renewed indefinitely a year later in the hope of a political agreement between representatives of the two communities. The organisation was represented by the Ulster Political Research Group who held talks with then Secretary of State Paul Murphy in November 2004.

At the time of writing, thirteen years after the ceasefires, loyalist paramilitaries had not yet decommissioned any of their weapons (except for a token gesture by the Loyalist Volunteer Force in 1998). Loyalist paramilitaries were also involved in violence and feuding between the different factions which ended in the autumn of 2005. In April 2004 the IMC linked the UDA to murders and criminal activity including drug dealing and in 2005 the Commission reported that the UVF remained active and involved in organised crime. In October 2006 the IMC reported that the UDA was 'active, violent and ruthless' and still involved in sectarian attacks with no sign of decommissioning, although there was some sign of the leadership trying to steer the organisation away from crime. There have also been claims of security force collusion with loyalist paramilitaries who acted as police informers. In January 2007 the Police Ombudsman Nuala O'Loan published a controversial and damning report on collusion between some members of the RUC Special Branch and members of the UVF who carried out sectarian murders and serious crimes in north Belfast during the 1990s.

....

✔ What you should have learnt from reading this chapter

- Northern Ireland has a party system that reflects the divisions along sectarian lines.

- There are two main parties in each bloc and important divisions exist within as well as between the nationalist and unionist blocs.

- Intra-party divisions, particularly within the UUP, have been important for the peace process as a whole.

- As exemplified by the Alliance Party, it is difficult for centre parties to attract substantial electoral support in the party system.

- In relation to paramilitary groups, there are tensions within the wider republican movement as evidenced by the existence of dissident republicans who have opposed the IRA ceasefire and the peace process.

🔎 Glossary of key terms

Abstentionism Sinn Féin's policy to boycott the parliaments in London, Dublin and Belfast; contest elections but not take seats; republicans viewed Stormont and Dáil Éireann as legislatures of illegitimate polities.
Decommissioning Process by which paramilitary groups give up their weapons; overseen by the Independent International Commission on Decommissioning.
Paramilitary A term given to illegal armed groups in Northern Ireland who used or continue to use political violence or the threat of violence to achieve political objectives.

? Likely examination questions

Discuss the dynamics of the party system in Northern Ireland.

How significant are intra-party divisions for politics in Northern Ireland?

Explain the role of paramilitary groups in Northern Ireland.

Helpful websites

Alliance Party of Northern Ireland: http://www.allianceparty.org

Democratic Unionist Party: http://www.dup.org.uk

Progressive Unionist Party: http://www.pup-ni.org.uk

Sinn Féin: http://www.sinnfein.ie

Social Democratic and Labour Party: http://www.sdlp.ie

Ulster Unionist Party: http://www.uup.org

Independent Monitoring Commission:
http://www.independentmonitoringcommission.org

 Suggestions for further reading

Steve Bruce, *God Save Ulster! The Religion and Politics of Paisleyism*, Oxford: Oxford University Press, 1986.

Feargal Cochrane, *Unionist Politics and the Politics of Unionism since the Anglo-Irish Agreement*, Cork: Cork University Press, 2001.

Richard English, *Armed Struggle: The History of the IRA*, Basingstoke: Macmillan, 2003.

Christopher Farrington, *Ulster Unionism and the Peace Process in Northern Ireland*, Basingstoke: Palgrave Macmillan, 2006.

Paul Mitchell and Rick Wilford, *Politics in Northern Ireland*, Oxford: Westview Press, 1999.

Gerard Murray, *John Hume and the SDLP: Impact and Survival in Northern Ireland*, Dublin: Irish Academic Press, 1998.

Henry Patterson, *Ireland Since 1939*, Dublin: Penguin Ireland, 2006.

CHAPTER 4

Finding a solution: from Sunningdale to the Framework Documents

Contents

Overview

This chapter explores the various attempts to resolve the conflict in Northern Ireland from the early 1970s to the mid-1990s. It begins with the collapse of Stormont and the introduction of direct rule in 1972. It then examines the successive attempts to find a solution to the conflict and political structures that could be supported by both nationalists and unionists. Each major initiative from the 1970s to the mid-1990s is examined with details on the substance of the proposals. It discusses the responses from the parties and shows why none of the initiatives in this period was able to command the support from both traditions.

Key issues to be covered in this chapter

- Political initiatives from the early 1970s to the 'peace process' of the 1990s
- Reactions to the various initiatives from the nationalist and unionist parties
- Why the attempts at finding a solution failed to garner support from both communities

Introduction of direct rule

The collapse of the Stormont regime in 1972 came about as a result of a combination of events over the previous four years. When Faulkner took over from Chichester-Clark as Prime Minister of Northern Ireland in 1971 he faced a challenging security situation due to the activities of the IRA, intra-communal violence, calls for reform from the civil rights movement, unionist opposition to 'appeasement' and the threat of British intervention.

The demise of Stormont was, therefore, due to a number of factors which weakened the Unionist Government and led to London assuming direct control. Certainly, the rise of the civil rights movement in the late 1960s played an important role in undermining the system. With an expanded Catholic middle class, Catholic political mobilisation called for an end to discrimination and an increased role in the state. As Chapter 2 outlined, the civil rights movement became increasingly about the nature of the state and changed its focus from state reform to criticism of state brutality. The unionist community ultimately felt threatened by these developments and pointed to the anti-partitionist rhetoric of civil rights campaigners. The situation became increasingly violent and was overtaken by street violence and sectarian clashes. Moreover, the security situation deteriorated with the re-emergence of the IRA following the republican split in December 1969 and the growth of paramilitary activity on both sides.

In the face of increased violence and mounting casualties, the Unionist Government was unable to uphold law and order. This situation led Chichester-Clark to seek assistance from the British Government and troops were dispatched to Northern Ireland in August 1969. However, the presence of British troops further alienated the minority community and did not prevent the growth of the IRA, with the army becoming targets for the republican armed campaign. As the violence continued in the early 1970s, Faulkner sought to introduce decisive measures to contain the situation and defeat the IRA; in August 1971 he introduced internment.

Internment, however, proved to be disastrous, providing a propaganda coup and recruitment tool for the IRA. Bew, Gibbon and Patterson note that Faulkner was 'reduced to increasingly desperate measures'.[1] In addition to introducing internment, he was also responsible for the decision to use live rather than rubber bullets to deal with the rioting in Londonderry on 30 January 1972. In what became known as 'Bloody Sunday', 13 civilians were killed by members of the British Parachute Regiment when violence broke out in the wake of a banned civil rights march against internment. As Bew, Gibbon and Patterson write, 'By February 1972 it was clear that far from creating the conditions for British engagement, Faulkner was creating a minor Vietnam'.[2]

The path to direct rule was also due to the difficulties faced by both Chichester-Clark and Faulkner in their attempts to deal with criticism from colleagues. Both prime ministers were concerned with the apparent threat of direct rule being imposed by Westminster. They appear to have introduced reforms in an effort to preserve the autonomy of the Northern Ireland state and prevent further intervention by Britain. This policy was contentious as it looked like appeasement to some Unionist Party colleagues and provoked opposition.

In the wake of internment and Bloody Sunday, British Prime Minister Heath's attention was increasingly drawn to the situation in Northern Ireland. The first three months of 1972 claimed eighty-seven deaths from the conflict and that year would be the worst year of 'the Troubles' in terms of lives lost – 470 deaths or 14 per cent of all deaths between 1969 and 1998.[3] Faulkner's handling of the situation, particularly the disastrous measure of internment, eventually provoked a response from the Tory Cabinet. It could be argued that the British Government took too long to intervene and introduce direct rule, and was slow to respond to the ineptitude of the Unionist Government over the four-year period from 1968. A crucial meeting between Heath and Faulkner took place in Downing Street on 22 March 1972, where, to Faulkner's surprise, the British Government moved to take control of security and law and order powers in Northern Ireland; this meant a complete transfer of security powers to Westminster. The following day, Stormont cabinet ministers were unanimous that they could not continue as a government and resigned, and the last sitting of the Stormont House of Commons took place on 28 March 1972.

The prorogation of Stormont on 1 April 1972 ended 50 years of unionist rule. Direct rule created a Northern Ireland Office with

William Whitelaw as Secretary of State for Northern Ireland and a ministerial team that would be responsible for Northern Ireland's departments. From Faulkner's perspective, he and his Unionist Party colleagues had been betrayed and humiliated by Heath's radical decision. The collapse of Stormont and introduction of direct rule then led to a period of unionist fragmentation with Ian Paisley and his Democratic Unionist Party posing the greatest threat to the Unionist Party.

Sunningdale Agreement and Executive 1973–4

The prorogation of Stormont and the introduction of direct rule in 1972 were to be a temporary arrangement. Deciding on the most appropriate institutional arrangement for devolved government with agreement among unionists and nationalists would prove extremely challenging. The British Government under Heath published a White Paper in March 1973, *Northern Ireland Constitutional Proposals* which proposed a devolved Assembly, executive power sharing between unionists and nationalists and a new institutional arrangement for cooperation with the Republic of Ireland. The idea of power sharing with nationalists rather than government by majority rule was a difficult prospect for many unionists. However, the proposed 'Irish dimension' in the form of new political structures was even more controversial as it would allow greater involvement for the Irish Government in the affairs of Northern Ireland. At the end of March the Ulster Unionist Council voted to accept the White Paper, although there were important tensions within the Unionist Party in relation to the establishment of a Council of Ireland.

The intra-unionist divisions became more evident following the June 1973 Northern Ireland Assembly election. There was considerable unionist fragmentation with five different unionist parties and groupings represented in the Assembly. A new party, the Vanguard Unionist Progressive Party was formed by William Craig following his failure to persuade the Ulster Unionist Council to reject the White Paper. As Bew, Gibbon and Patterson outline, anti-White Paper unionists predominated with 34.5 per cent of the total vote and twenty-seven seats compared with the Faulknerites' 26.5 per cent and twenty-three seats.[4] The SDLP won 22 per cent of the vote and nineteen seats and the Alliance Party obtained 9 per cent of the vote and eight seats.

In October 1973 the Secretary of State, William Whitelaw called the parties to Stormont to begin a series of inter-party negotiations on the formation of a power-sharing executive. The delegations included representatives from the UUP, the SDLP and the Alliance Party. On 23 October 1973 a committee of the UUP voted by 132 to 105 to support the party taking part in a future executive. However, as Patterson notes, Faulkner 'seriously overestimated his ability to sell the prospective deal to his party'.[5] Opposition to the proposed political arrangements grew within the unionist community, and Faulkner's position was made even more difficult by the insistence of the SDLP delegation, particularly John Hume, for a Council of Ireland with substantial powers. On 21 November, the parties agreed to set up a power-sharing executive consisting of eleven members: six Unionist Party; four SDLP and one Alliance member.

Sunningdale conference
From 6 to 9 December 1973 the parties and the two governments attended a conference at Sunningdale, Berkshire, England to resolve the outstanding issues on the setting up of the executive and to reach agreement on the Council of Ireland. The delegations included the Unionist Party, the SDLP and the Alliance Party and the British Prime Minister Edward Heath and the Irish Taoiseach Liam Cosgrave. Patterson writes that the Sunningdale Conference 'was an unmitigated disaster for Faulkner's standing in the unionist community'.[6] The SDLP continued to push the proposed Council of Ireland as the focus of the negotiations, which was to consist of a Council of Ministers and a Consultative Assembly. The Council of Ministers would include seven members from the Northern Ireland Executive and seven members from the Irish Government. The institution was to have executive and harmonising functions, although its actual powers were set aside as the subject of future discussions. The Consultative Assembly was to be made up of thirty members from the Northern Ireland Assembly and thirty members from Dáil Éireann. A communiqué was issued on 9 December announcing that agreement had been reached at Sunningdale and that the Council of Ireland would be created.

A power-sharing government

On 1 January 1974 the Northern Ireland Executive took office with the UUP's Brian Faulkner as Chief Executive and the SDLP's Gerry Fitt as Deputy Chief Executive. This was Northern Ireland's first power-sharing government between unionists and nationalists. However, just a few days later, on 4 January, the Ulster Unionist Council voted to reject the Council of Ireland as proposed in the Sunningdale communiqué and Brian Faulkner resigned as party leader. A further challenge for the Northern Ireland Executive parties arose with the UK general election on 28 February 1974. In Northern Ireland the election was pushed by the parties as a referendum on power sharing and the Council of Ireland. Significantly, parties in support of the Executive competed against one another.

In contrast, the parties opposed to Sunningdale were more effective as a cohesive political group. The DUP, Vanguard, the Orange Order and 600 delegates from Unionist Party constituency associations made a political pact and formed the United Ulster Unionist Council with the slogan 'Dublin is just a Sunningdale away'. In a devastating result for the Executive, candidates in opposition to Sunningdale won eleven of the twelve Westminster seats. The election saw a narrow Labour victory with Harold Wilson becoming Prime Minister and Merlyn Rees became Secretary of State for Northern Ireland.

The results of the 1974 general election were extremely damaging for the Northern Ireland Executive. As Patterson comments, 'The Executive had lost all legitimacy with the bulk of the Unionist electorate, and this is the key to understanding the British Government's reaction to the unprecedented industrial action by the Ulster Workers' Council (UWC), which was the occasion, but not the fundamental cause, of the Executive's collapse'.[7] The UWC was formed in November 1973 by groups of loyalist trade unionists. It had clear links with the main loyalist paramilitary organisations and its coordinating committee included UDA and UVF members. The UWC strike began on 14 May 1974 and saw the main industries shut down, roads closed and barricades erected. The UWC even took control of the Ballylumford power station at Larne, threatening the provision of electricity. Arguably the Northern Ireland Executive was already doomed due to the February election results and internal divisions over the Council of Ireland. The crisis came to a head two weeks later, leading Brian Faulkner to resign as Chief Executive and bringing the power-sharing government to an end.

Rolling devolution 1982

Following the failure of the Sunningdale power-sharing experiment, the British government continued to explore an alternative way forward. Harold Wilson's Labour Government then organised elections to a Constitutional Convention which would consider the most appropriate political arrangements for Northern Ireland to be agreed between the parties. The election to the Constitutional Convention was held on 1 May 1975 and the UUP won 25.4 per cent of the vote, the DUP obtained 14.8 per cent and the Vanguard Unionist Party won 12.7 per cent. These three parties and an independent represented the United Ulster Unionist Council with forty-eight out of the seventy-eight seats. A report of the Convention was published in November 1975 and included the United Ulster Unionist Council proposals for a return to majority rule at Stormont, which were rejected by the SDLP, the Alliance Party and the British Government. Without agreement among the parties, Secretary of State Merlyn Rees announced the closure of the Convention in March 1976.

The 1979 General Election returned a Conservative Government with Margaret Thatcher as Prime Minister. A new round of inter-party talks was then launched by Secretary of State Humphrey Atkins in November 1979. However, the talks failed to make progress for a number of reasons: the UUP did not take part; the DUP preferred majority rule for any new Stormont government; and the SDLP wanted to pursue the 'Irish dimension'. Although the Atkins talks were more about achieving some level of consensus rather than an overall settlement, the initiative collapsed a year later without agreement between the parties.

In September 1981 Atkins was replaced by James Prior as Secretary of State for Northern Ireland. Prior was keen to get the political process moving, end direct rule and agree a system of devolved government whereby local politicians would take control. In 1982 Prior proposed elections to a new assembly and a new approach known as 'rolling devolution'. Under Prior's proposals the new assembly would initially have a consultative and scrutiny role but not legislative power. It would then be up to the elected representatives to decide on how powers would be devolved from Westminster and an agreed way forward would require support from 70 per cent of assembly members. The devolution of power from Westminster to Northern Ireland would, therefore, take place in stages, hence the term 'rolling devolution'. If the assembly could demonstrate that it could work on a 'cross-community' basis then its role would increase to include legislative and executive devolution.

In relation to the unionist response to Prior's agenda, the UUP was opposed to the idea of 'rolling devolution', particularly the faction within the party which preferred the integration of Northern Ireland into the UK rather than devolution. The party participated intermittently in Prior's Assembly. Moreover, the UUP and DUP were opposed to the concept of power sharing with nationalists. With regard to the nationalist perspective, the SDLP rejected Prior's proposals as they failed to provide an 'Irish dimension'. The party, therefore, boycotted the initiative; it would contest the election but on an abstentionist platform as elected members would not take their seats. Sinn Féin also contested the 1982 Assembly Election in a number of constituencies to oppose the SDLP, also on an abstentionist platform.

1982 Assembly election

At the 1982 Assembly election, the main parties polled as follows: UUP 29.7 per cent of the vote and twenty-six seats; DUP 23 per cent and twenty-one seats; SDLP 18.8 per cent and fourteen seats; Sinn Féin 10.1 per cent and five seats; and Alliance 9.3 per cent and ten seats.[8] This was a good result for the UUP and the DUP. The election results also pointed to the emergence of Sinn Féin as a political force which would potentially pose a major threat to the position of the SDLP as the largest nationalist party. As Bew, Gibbon and Patterson note 'Fears of the imminent demise of constitutional nationalism became commonplace in London and Dublin'.[9] The new Northern Ireland Assembly opened on 11 November 1982 but the SDLP and Sinn Féin did not take their seas. The Assembly officially lasted until 23 June 1986, but could not have succeeded given the SDLP's refusal to participate; Prior's plan for the assembly to demonstrate its 'cross-community' credentials was, therefore, impossible.

Prior's initiative was clearly not going to lead to agreement among the parties as the SDLP refused to take their seats in the Assembly. The SDLP felt that Prior's 'rolling devolution' scheme was bound to fail as it focused on achieving a purely internal solution and did not include the party's all-important 'Irish dimension'. Another factor for the SDLP was the perception that Sinn Féin was growing as a political force and it was afraid of losing out to Sinn Féin in the competition for which party was the strongest voice of Northern nationalism. The Prior Assembly met further difficulties as some within the UUP preferred further integration of Northern Ireland rather than devolution, and the unionist parties were opposed to power sharing with nationalists.

Anglo-Irish Agreement 1985

The Anglo-Irish Agreement (AIA) was the most significant political initiative in Northern Ireland since the Sunningdale communiqué. The AIA was the product of five years of diplomatic negotiations between Britain and Ireland which commenced not long after Margaret Thatcher became British Prime Minister in 1979. For instance, summit meetings were held in May and December 1980 between Thatcher and Taoiseach Charles Haughey which led to a period of increased cooperation between the two governments. A Fine Gael government came to power in the Republic of Ireland in 1981 with Garret FitzGerald becoming Taoiseach. At a summit between Thatcher and FitzGerald in November the two premiers decided to establish an Anglo-Irish Intergovernmental Council for regular meetings on issues of mutual concern.

Why did the British Government adopt a new approach?

It is important to note that there were multiple factors that led the British government to embark on a new approach to Northern Ireland at this time. As Bew, Gibbon and Patterson comment 'the emergence of an apparently dangerous level of political support for republicanism and Haughey's replacement at the end of 1982 by the more accommodating FitzGerald created the circumstances for a radical departure in British policy'.[10] Due to the failure of previous initiatives the British government began to look for an alternative way forward. For Thatcher, there was need for a policy initiative that would be accepted by the Irish government and she wanted more cooperation with Dublin in relation to security and intelligence. For FitzGerald, something needed to be done about the potential growth of Sinn Féin and he sought to shore up the position of the SDLP and constitutional nationalism against militant republicanism. Significantly, while the SDLP received information from the Irish government on the discussions, unionists were excluded from the development of negotiations.

The AIA was signed on 15 November 1985 by Margaret Thatcher and Garret FitzGerald. Article 1 of the AIA affirmed that any change in the status of Northern Ireland would only come about with the consent of a majority of the people of Northern Ireland. The document recognised that the present wish of the majority of people was for Northern Ireland to remain within the UK; but the document also suggested that the British Government would facilitate Irish unification if that was the wish of a majority in the future. This was a reiteration of the '**consent principle**' which was introduced in the Sunningdale communiqué of 1973.

New role for the Irish Government

Significantly, the AIA meant a special role for the Republic of Ireland in the governance of Northern Ireland. It established an Anglo-Irish Intergovernmental Conference jointly chaired by the Secretary of State for Northern Ireland and the Irish Minister for Foreign Affairs. Under Article 2 the Irish Government would have a consultative role in the affairs of Northern Ireland. This was to be related to security matters, legal affairs and the promotion of cross-border cooperation. Under Article 3 the Inter-Governmental Conference would be serviced by a joint secretariat of British and Irish officials based in Belfast. Article 4 of the AIA confirmed the two governments' preference for devolution as the most appropriate political structure. The document stated that devolved structures should secure widespread acceptance throughout the community and that a local administration would require the cooperation of political representatives of both traditions. This position clearly meant power sharing between nationalists and unionists.

Parties' reactions to the AIA

The unionist community was united in opposition to the AIA, particularly in relation to the increased role for the Irish Government in the affairs of Northern Ireland. The 'Irish dimension', which was so important for the SDLP, had too much significance for unionism. The unionist parties were also aggrieved as they had not been consulted about what was contained in the agreement before its publication. Unionists, therefore, felt they had been betrayed by Thatcher. As Cochrane observes, 'the realization dawned on many unionists in November 1985 that they remained part of the United Kingdom in sufferance, a residue of Britain's imperial past and a diplomatic loose-end yet to be tied up'.[11]

In response, the unionist parties launched a joint campaign against the agreement. There was a considerable sense of cohesion within the unionist community in opposition to the AIA under the 'Ulster Says No' banner. On 19 November the eighteen district councils controlled by unionist parties voted for a policy of adjournment against the agreement. On 23 November a rally was held at Belfast City Hall, organised by unionist parties and attended by more than 100,000 people. On 17 December the fifteen unionist MPs resigned their Westminster seats in protest at the AIA. A series of by-elections were then held on 23 January 1986 where unionist parties increased their share of the vote from that of the 1983 general election. And in February 1986 local councils with a unionist majority voted to refuse to set the local government tax. The AIA had also made irrelevant the failed Prior Assembly which was eventually dissolved in June 1986.

In contrast, the AIA was received much more positively by the SDLP. As Murray and Tonge point out, 'The Anglo-Irish Agreement started the process which the SDLP had outlined for joint government action in Northern Ireland'.[12] The document echoed the SDLP analysis that any settlement in Northern Ireland would not be simply an internal affair but would have to involve the Irish Government. There was also acknowledgement of the legitimacy of nationalist identity, grievances and aspirations. While Sinn Féin publicly rejected the AIA on the basis that it maintained partition of the island there were some divergent internal interpretations within the party. Sinn Féin's assessment of the agreement was that 'cosmetic internal reform and a powerless consultative role would be offered to Dublin and [to] the SDLP in return for their active assistance in creating political stability in the Six Counties'.[13]

Brooke–Mayhew talks 1991–2

The appointment of Peter Brooke as Secretary of State for Northern Ireland in July 1989 marked a new departure for politics in Northern Ireland. Brooke had already made a number of important speeches to clarify the British Government's position on Northern Ireland. For instance, he explained that the British presence in Northern Ireland was due to the wish of a majority to remain within the UK and he appeared to speak to republicans when he stated that 'it is not the aspiration to a sovereign, united Ireland, against which we set our face, but its violent expression'.[14] He also spoke of Britain's lack of 'selfish strategic or economic interests in Northern Ireland' which rejected the republican argument about British imperialism. Brooke then launched a new initiative in search of an agreement between nationalists and unionists through inter-party talks.

To secure unionist participation in the talks Brooke provided for a suspension of the Anglo-Irish Intergovernmental Conference Secretariat for a fixed period. The talks were attended by the UUP, the DUP, the SDLP and Alliance. The Secretary of State structured the talks under three strands: Strand One would focus on the internal arrangements in Northern Ireland; Strand Two would look at north–south relations; and Strand Three would centre on east–west relations between Britain and the Republic of Ireland. The talks were delayed by several months and failed to make any real progress once they got up and running. Certainly, there was a distinct lack of trust between the two unionist parties and the SDLP.

The UUP and the DUP had a common negotiating position in the talks. The two unionist parties proposed an assembly with non-executive responsibilities run by a number of proportional committees. With a larger assembly, the unionists were confident they would be able to secure political control of the committees. The unionists' proposals were certainly not enough for the SDLP who advocated full executive power sharing and an Irish dimension. As noted by Cochrane, 'This was not a power-sharing relationship in the sense that nationalists understood that term and consequently held little attraction for the SDLP'.[15]

Following the failure to achieve a breakthrough between the parties under Brooke, the talks continued under the new Secretary of State Sir Patrick Mayhew in July 1992. As Bew, Gibbon and Patterson comment on unionist participation: 'The Unionists approached the talks in a slightly more confident frame of mind: their proposals were certainly more advanced and elaborate'.[16] Although the unionists were prepared to consider proportionality in new political structures, this would not stretch to full executive power sharing. In relation to the SDLP proposals, the party argued for a form of joint authority between Britain and Ireland with a European dimension. The party's paper proposed a collective presidency with six members: one representative from the British Government, the Irish Government and the European Union, respectively and three members elected in Northern Ireland.

The unionists were vehemently opposed to the SDLP's proposed involvement of the Irish Government and the EU. The talks were ultimately deadlocked over the parties' divergent positions in relation to the internal arrangements for governing Northern Ireland. Nevertheless, as Murray and Tonge point out, the Brooke–Mayhew talks were significant as they provided a vehicle for the parties to exchange ideas and 'set in place a mechanism for dialogue between the divergent sides on an equal footing, something absent since the collapse of the Sunningdale experiment in 1974'.[17]

Downing Street Declaration 1993

The failure of the Brooke–Mayhew talks between the local political parties led the British Government to pursue an intergovernmental approach with the Republic of Ireland. It is important to note that dialogue between the SDLP and Sinn Féin informed this intergovernmental approach. Although talks between the SDLP and Sinn Féin had ended in 1988 without progress, John Hume and Gerry Adams re-commenced their discussion in 1993 and published a number of statements. The first and key statement was published in April 1993 whereby the two party leaders agreed that an internal settlement would not be a solution of the conflict. The statement is significant in relation to what Hume and Adams stated with regard to Irish national **self-determination**:

We accept that the Irish people as a whole have a right to national self-determination. This is a view shared by a majority of the people of this island though not by all its people. The exercise of self-determination is a matter for agreement between the people of Ireland. It is the search for that agreement and the means of achieving it on which we will be concentrating.

Intergovernmental discussions between British Prime Minister John Major and Taoiseach Albert Reynolds led to the publication of the *Joint Declaration on Peace: the Downing Street Declaration* (DSD) in December 1993. As Bew, Gibbon and Patterson point out, 'The Downing Street Declaration proved to be a document of considerable originality and sophistication'.[18] The document stated that both Governments 'recognise that the ending of divisions can come about only through the agreement and co-operation of the people, North and South, representing both traditions in Ireland'. The DSD reiterated the 'consent principle' by stating that the British Government 'will uphold the democratic wish of the greater number of the people of Northern Ireland on the issue of whether they prefer to support the Union or a sovereign united Ireland'. The British Government reiterated a comment made by Peter Brooke in 1990 that it had 'no selfish strategic or economic interest in Northern Ireland'.[19]

The DSD also tackled the issue of the right to self-determination:

> The British Government agree that it is for the people of the island of Ireland alone, by agreement between the two parts respectively, to exercise their right of self-determination on the basis of consent, freely and concurrently given, North and South, to bring about a united Ireland, if that is their wish.

This statement meant that the people of Northern Ireland would determine consent or rejection of a change in constitutional status. On behalf of the Taoiseach the document stated:

> it would be wrong to attempt to impose a united Ireland, in the absence of the freely given consent of the majority of the people of Northern Ireland. He accepts, on behalf of the Irish Government, that the democratic right of self-determination by the people of Ireland as a whole must be achieved and exercised with and subject to the agreement and consent of a majority of the people of Northern Ireland.

This statement recognised that a united Ireland would not take place without the consent of the unionist community as the majority in Northern Ireland (the 'consent principle'). However, the DSD also stated that if a future majority vote for Irish unity then both governments would support and give legislative effect to that constitutional change. The DSD also held out some potential for republicans to become involved in agreeing a way forward in a process of political dialogue with the two Governments and the other parties:

> democratically mandated parties which establish a commitment to exclusively peaceful methods and which have shown that they abide by the democratic process, are free to participate fully in democratic politics and to join in dialogue in due course between the Governments and the political parties on the way ahead.[20]

Significance of the Downing Street Declaration

The DSD was a significant political initiative as it confirmed the consent principle whereby Irish unity would come about only with the agreement of a majority in Northern Ireland. This was very different to how republicans had approached the idea of Irish national self-determination on the basis of the island of Ireland. As Hennessey comments the DSD 'enshrined the Unionist veto. It also marked the point at which constitutional Nationalism in Ireland finally embraced the principle of consent on Unionist terms and abandoned previous hopes of manoeuvring the British into becoming persuaders for a united Ireland'.[21] The republican movement was thus disappointed with the DSD. Sinn Féin President Gerry Adams complained that the DSD 'does not set any timetable for a united Ireland. It does not commit the people of Northern Ireland to join a united Ireland against their wishes, and it does not establish any arrangement for joint authority'.[22] For a number of months Sinn Féin sought further clarification and finally rejected the document in July 1994.

Although the DSD confirmed the consent principle in a form acceptable to unionism, the unionist community was nevertheless suspicious of the language of Irish self-determination. Major was, therefore, compelled to reassure unionists that the Declaration confirmed Northern Ireland's place within the United Kingdom so long as a majority of people wished it. He pointed to the Declaration's statement on self-determination and claimed that it 'protects the position of the majority in Northern Ireland, and means that change can only come about with their consent'.[23] However, a vociferous response came from the DUP as details emerged of the British Government's contact with the IRA in the early 1990s. For Paisley the DSD was a tripartite agreement between Major, Reynolds and the IRA which 'sold Ulster to buy off the fiendish republican scum'.[24]

Framework Documents 1995

A new political situation was born following the IRA ceasefire in August 1994 and the Combined Loyalist Military Command ceasefire announced in October. The ceasefires opened the door to a new departure towards fully inclusive dialogue. The two governments wanted to get inter-party talks back on track along the same lines as the Brooke–Mayhew talks of 1991–2 with a three strand approach. In the wake of the ceasefires the British and Irish Governments also wanted to open up the way for republicans to be included in the negotiations.

The British and Irish Governments published their 'Frameworks for the Future' on 17 February 1995. The 'Framework Documents' consisted of two documents: Part One was the British Government's *The Framework Documents – A Framework for Accountable Government in Northern Ireland*; and Part Two was the British and Irish Governments' *The Framework Documents – A New Framework for Agreement*. Both documents had their origin in the failed Brooke–Mayhew talks of 1991–2. Part One, *A Framework for Accountable Government in Northern Ireland* presented the British Government's proposals for internal political structures. The proposals included a ninety-member assembly elected by proportional representation and an executive 'panel' as a kind of collective presidency of 'probably' three members.

Part Two, *A New Framework for Agreement* was published on behalf of the two governments and addressed north–south and east–west relations. In relation to north–south relations, the document was significant as it proposed a north–south body which would discharge functions on an all-Ireland or cross-border basis. It would have functions in consultative, harmonising and executive categories. The proposals in relation to east–west relations recommended the establishment of an Intergovernmental Conference similar to that under the Anglo-Irish Agreement of 1985. This body would ensure that north–south cooperation would continue even in the event that devolved institutions ceased to operate and direct rule were to be restored. The Framework Documents also included an endorsement of Irish self-determination to be based on a majority in Northern Ireland who would decide on whether to remain in the UK or opt to join a sovereign united Ireland.

Parties' reactions to the Framework Documents

In response to the Framework Documents the unionist parties were opposed to the extent of north–south cooperation envisaged. They were concerned at the proposals for cross-border cooperation and were opposed to any statutory north–south political institution with powers to be administered uniformly throughout Ireland. Unionists also rejected the British–Irish Intergovernmental Conference which they feared would introduce joint authority in Northern Ireland. It appears that the UUP leader James Molyneaux did not envisage that the British Government would propose political institutions that would be more acceptable to nationalists. To his party colleagues he had taken for granted the party's relationship with the Major Government. This situation created difficulties for Molyneaux's leadership leading to his resignation as party leader in August 1995 and replacement by David Trimble.

Nationalists were more positive in their response to the Framework Documents. The SDLP was prepared to progress negotiations on the basis of the text. With regard to the Sinn Féin response, Gerry Adams claimed: 'The ethos of the document is clearly an all-island one. It deals with the general concept of one-island social, economic and political structures, and moves the situation closer to an all-island settlement'.[25] However, Sinn Féin did not support arrangements for a new administration at Stormont and wanted the two governments to establish all-Ireland institutions with immediate effect. Republicans were also somewhat disappointed that the IRA ceasefire announced in August 1994 and the publication of the Framework Documents had not yet led to Sinn Féin being part of inter-party talks. However, despite these differences the Documents were a significant part of the process towards inter-party talks and agreement on the structures of devolved power sharing in Northern Ireland.

Table 4.1   Political initiatives 1973–95

Initiative	Proposals	Unionist reaction	Nationalist/ Republican reaction
Sunningdale 1973–4	Power-sharing executive at Stormont; Council of Ireland with executive power	Ulster Unionist Council voted to reject the Council of Ireland and Faulkner resigned as party leader	'Irish dimension' in form of Council of Ireland vital for SDLP; Sinn Féin excluded
Atkins talks 1979	Talks to achieve some level of consensus; failed to make progress	UUP did not take part; DUP preferred majority rule at Stormont	SDLP committed to 'Irish dimension'; Sinn Féin excluded
Prior Assembly 1982–6	Talks to agree system of devolved government and a scheme of 'rolling devolution'	Faction within the UUP preferred integration rather than devolution; UUP participated intermittently; DUP also opposed to power sharing	SDLP boycotted the initiative as it lacked an 'Irish dimension'; Sinn Féin also contested 1982 election on abstentionist platform
Anglo-Irish Agreement 1985	Enhanced role for Irish government via Anglo-Irish Intergovernmental Conference	Outright opposition, intra-unionist pact	SDLP accepted as basis for future discussions
Brooke– Mayhew talks 1991–2	Inter-party talks on political structures failed due to mistrust	UUP and DUP proposed assembly with proportional	SDLP committed to full executive power sharing and an 'Irish

Table 4.1   *(cont.)*

Initiative	Proposals	Unionist reaction	Nationalist/ Republican reaction
		committees but without executive power	dimension'; Sinn Féin excluded
Downing Street Declaration 1993	Irish self-determination on the basis of consent, north and south; meant that Irish unity would not take place without unionist support	Suspicious of language of Irish self-determination; DUP accused Major of 'treachery'	Rejected by Sinn Féin as it meant no change to Northern Ireland's constitutional status
Framework Documents 1995	Internal structures: ninety-member assembly, executive panel; north–south body; British–Irish Intergovernmental Conference	Opposed north–south body with executive power and rejected British–Irish Intergovernmental Conference	SDLP prepared to progress negotiations; Sinn Féin opposed to Stormont administration and wanted all-Ireland bodies immediately

 What you should have learnt from reading this chapter

- Since the start of 'the Troubles' in Northern Ireland successive attempts have been made by the British and Irish Governments to end the conflict and bring about agreement between nationalists and unionists.

- Over the years political initiatives included inter-party talks among the local political parties and documents published by the two governments.

- The political initiatives from the 1970s to the mid-1990s failed to secure a settlement as they were not sufficient to secure support from both traditions. A successful initiative thus needed to secure the satisfaction of both communities.

Glossary of key terms

Consent principle A majority in Northern Ireland to decide on whether to remain within the United Kingdom or approve a united Ireland.
Self-determination The right of a nation to decide on how they are to be governed.

Likely examination question

Why did successive political initiatives fail to secure agreement between nationalists and unionists?

Helpful websites

Conflict Archive on the Internet: http://www.cain.ulst.ac.uk

Northern Ireland Elections: http://www.ark.ac.uk/elections

Suggestions for further reading

Paul Bew, Peter Gibbon and Henry Patterson, *Northern Ireland 1921/2001 Political Forces and Social Classes*, London: Serif, 2002.

Thomas Hennessey, *The Northern Ireland Peace Process: Ending the Troubles?*, Dublin: Gill and Macmillan, 2000.

Gerard Murray and Jonathan Tonge, *Sinn Féin and the SDLP: From Alienation to Participation*, Dublin: O'Brien Press, 2005.

British and Irish Government Policy

Contents

Overview

The chapter analyses the policy of the British and Irish Governments towards Northern Ireland and their respective contributions to the peace process. It explores the role of the British state in the conflict and the Irish state's former territorial claim to Northern Ireland. It traces the policies of successive administrations, the context of British–Irish relations and the relationship of London and Dublin with both unionism and nationalism. The chapter provides an overall assessment of British and Irish Government policy throughout the 1990s peace process and the signing of the Good Friday Agreement. The final sub-section outlines how the two governments worked together over the years and the convergence of their positions following the suspension of the devolved institutions in October 2002 leading to restored devolved power sharing in May 2007.

Key issues to be covered in this chapter

- The role of the British and Irish Governments in the Northern Ireland conflict
- The relationship between the British and Irish Governments and nationalism and unionism, respectively
- The convergence of the two governments' position in recent years
- The centrality of the two governments in bringing about agreement among the parties

The British Government: cause of the conflict or neutral arbiter?

The traditional view held by republicans is that the Northern Ireland conflict came about as a result of a series of actions by the British state. To illustrate this contention republicans look to the Government of Ireland Act 1920 and the partition of the island as evidence of disastrous acts by the British Government which inevitably led to conflict. As we saw in Chapter 2, the partition of Ireland created Northern Ireland and the division of the province of Ulster excluding Cavan, Donegal and Monaghan. For republicans, then, the conflict was a consequence of partition and the creation of Northern Ireland or the 'six-counties' was viewed as illegitimate. For instance, Sinn Féin's Martin McGuinness, speaking in 1992 expressed this view: 'The reason, in our analysis, why the situation is the way it is in this part of Ireland is primarily because of all that the British Government has done in this part of Ireland, and its failure to address its responsibility in all that has happened . . .'[1]

Republicans have also claimed that Britain's presence in Ireland was a result of British imperialist interests. In other words, Britain was involved in Northern Ireland for self-interested political and economic reasons. Republicans were also of the view that successive British Governments were concerned to placate unionists and that they were reluctant to make decisions against unionists. Moreover, republicans felt that Britain consistently granted unionists a veto on political change, thereby adding to the conflict and preventing a solution. Republicans also pointed to British Government security policies in Northern Ireland and the actions of the British army and local security forces as evidence of Britain's responsibility for the conflict. Thus, the traditional republican view held that the conflict would come to an end only with British withdrawal from Ireland.

Importantly, the view that Britain was the cause of the conflict in Northern Ireland was not shared by the SDLP. As McGarry and O'Leary point out, SDLP leader John Hume argued that since the signing of the Anglo-Irish Agreement (AIA) in 1985 the British Government became formally neutral on the constitutional status of Northern Ireland.[2] The SDLP saw in the AIA an explicit recognition of the nationalist community in Northern Ireland and a commitment to Anglo-Irish intergovernmental relations as central to finding a solution. Murray and Tonge note the significance of the AIA for the SDLP analysis of the conflict and aspirations of the nationalist community: 'it clarified the responsibility of the two governments to act as referees for the implementation of power-sharing in any new devolved system of government in Northern Ireland'.[3]

In 1988, SDLP leader John Hume embarked on a series of meetings with Sinn Féin President Gerry Adams. In these discussions Hume stressed his view that the British Government should not be viewed by nationalists and republicans as an obstacle to unity. Hume's view was that Britain was now formally neutral and that the British Government would not prevent or stand in the way of Irish unity subject to popular support. The result of the dialogue between the SDLP and Sinn Féin in the early 1990s formed what became known as the 'Hume–Adams' document. The statement called on the British Government to 'use all its influence and energy to win the consent of a majority in Northern Ireland' for agreed independent structures for the island as a whole based on Irish self-determination.[4] In other words, Hume and Adams hoped that the British Government (then under John Major) would agree to persuade unionists to consent to Irish unity. The view that Britain should act as a persuader for Irish unity was also found in Sinn Féin's 1992 document, *Towards a Lasting Peace in Ireland*. Murray and Tonge note that the document did not set a timetable for British withdrawal and this meant a shift in policy towards the British state.[5] However, the authors also note that it is unclear whether the Sinn Féin leadership ever really believed that Britain would seek to persuade unionists to consent to a united Ireland.

How have successive British Governments viewed their role in Northern Ireland?

It is important to consider whether the British state viewed its role in Northern Ireland as either a party to the conflict or as a neutral arbiter. In relation to the republican view of the British partition of Ireland, McGarry and O'Leary point out that in both the Government of Ireland Act 1920 and the Anglo-Irish Treaty 1921 'the British government envisaged eventual agreement on Irish unity and self-government – albeit with the "Empire" '.[6] It is also important to consider whether the British state was responsible for the problems associated with the Stormont regime from 1920 until the outbreak of 'the Troubles'. McGarry and O'Leary write that the British government's role during this time 'is better understood as that of indirect responsibility through semi-deliberate neglect . . . The control actually established by the Ulster Unionist Party between 1920 and 1972 was not planned, but rather was sanctioned by the neglect of successive British governments'.[7]

It is clear that the British state was largely reactive to events in Northern Ireland at the end of the 1960s. As Bew, Gibbon and Patterson state, 'British intervention in August 1969 was planned and executed as the minimum possible form of intervention by the British state . . . Every effort seems to have been to forestall military intervention, and then to minimise and terminate it'.[8] Despite statements made by Harold Wilson in favour of Irish unity and British withdrawal, British Governments opted to pursue a strategy whereby parties would agree to new institutional structures, as evidenced by Secretary of State for Northern Ireland William Whitelaw's efforts in relation to the Sunningdale communiqué of 1973. In the 1980s the British Government under Margaret Thatcher was first and foremost concerned with defeating the IRA. Her policy position, and cooperation with the Irish Republic, was derived from a belief that more security and intelligence was needed to defeat the IRA.

Shift in British policy

A shift in British policy came at the end of the 1980s and early 1990s in the context of signs that the republican movement was reappraising its strategy. In response to these developments the British Government sought to try to facilitate this transition so that the IRA would abandon its campaign of violence. This period also saw a number of key speeches delivered by British ministers who sought to clarify Britain's role and responsibilities in Northern Ireland. For instance, Secretary of State for Northern Ireland Peter Brooke made a highly significant speech in November 1990. The speech was clearly aimed at republicans and pointed to the 'Britishness' of the unionist population in Northern Ireland which Sinn Féin had failed to acknowledge. Importantly, Brooke stressed that the British Government had no objection to the principle of Irish unity, but was opposed to the use of violence by the IRA in its objective of bringing about a united Ireland.

Brooke's speech had the intention of refuting the republican interpretation about the role and responsibility of the British state for the conflict. He sought to emphasise that it was not credible for republicans to accuse Britain of imperialist intentions in Northern Ireland. As outlined in the next section, the British Government under John Major took on the role of trying to encourage republicans to embark on mainstream politics leading to a common approach with the Irish Government and the signing of the Downing Street Declaration in 1993.

It can be argued that the approach of successive British Governments has been one of pragmatism. An incremental approach has been adopted whereby successive British Governments have awarded concessions or 'carrots' to the respective parties throughout the peace process. This conscious effort to trade concessions with nationalism/republicanism and unionism has been particularly evident under the Blair administrations. Certainly, the Labour victory at the 1997 general election with Tony Blair becoming Prime Minister proved a catalyst for securing agreement. Indeed, it has been a particular focus for the Blair Government to portray the British state as 'neutral' and a facilitator in the process with the outcome to be agreed by the local parties. However, at times Blair's Government was accused of going too far to comfort republicans while not appreciating the difficulties on the unionist side. For instance, Blair was criticised for not pushing republicans on decommissioning and failing to acknowledge the challenges experienced by former UUP leader David Trimble in the wake of the 1998 Agreement. Interestingly, such criticism was expressed by former Secretary of State for Northern Ireland Peter Mandelson, who said that to keep the process on track Blair would give consideration to republican demands which Mandelson viewed as excessive and risked alienating unionists.[9]

Successive British Governments have clearly viewed their contribution as that of a 'third-party' in the peace process where their role has been to drive an inter-governmental approach alongside successive Irish Governments. Thus, a key theme of the 1990s and particularly since 1998 has been the 'partnership' between the two governments. This common purpose was evident to an extent between

Table 5.1 British Prime Ministers and Secretaries of State for Northern Ireland 1968–2008

Year	British Prime Minister	Secretary of State for Northern Ireland	Party
1964–June 1970	Harold Wilson	James Callaghan	Labour
June 1970–May 1974	Edward Heath	Reginald Maudling William Whitelaw Francis Pym	Conservative
February 1974–May 1979	Harold Wilson February 1974–1976 James Callaghan 1976–May 1979	Merlyn Rees Roy Mason	Labour
May 1979–June 1983	Margaret Thatcher	Humphrey Atkins James Prior	Conservative
June 1983–June 1987	Margaret Thatcher	James Prior Douglas Hurd Tom King	Conservative
June 1987–April 1992	Margaret Thatcher June 1997–November 1990 John Major November 1990–April 1992	Tom King Peter Brooke	Conservative
April 1992–May 1997	John Major	Patrick Mayhew	Conservative
May 1997–June 2001	Tony Blair	Mo Mowlam Peter Mandelson John Reid	Labour
June 2001–May 2005	Tony Blair	John Reid Paul Murphy	Labour
May 2005–June 2007	Tony Blair	Peter Hain	Labour
June 2007–	Gordon Brown	Shaun Woodward	Labour

Source: www.cain.ulst.ac.uk/ /issues/politics/secretary/tabgov.htm.

Thatcher and FitzGerald in relation to the Anglo-Irish Agreement of 1985, Major and Reynolds with the Downing Street Declaration of 1993 and particularly between Blair and Ahern since 1998. Indeed, the relationship between Blair and Ahern was extremely productive following the suspension of the devolved institutions in 2002, whereby the two governments threatened the implementation of a 'Plan B' in the form of additional London–Dublin cooperation in the absence of inter-party agreement on power sharing.

The British Government and republicanism

From the outbreak of 'the Troubles' the British Government became increasingly involved in trying to restore law and order. For the British state, ending the conflict was first and foremost about defeating the IRA. It was felt that victory over the IRA could be achieved by military means with enhanced powers for the security forces. For instance, the policy of 'Ulsterisation' in the 1970s was implemented whereby the security response would be handled by the locally recruited Royal Ulster Constabulary (RUC) and Ulster Defence Regiment (UDR). The 'Troubles' continued, however, amid a vicious circle of the IRA attempting to bring about British withdrawal and the British Government seeking to defeat militant republicans. Thus, the difficult relationship between republicans and the British Government was of central importance to the ongoing conflict, particularly as contact increased between the two sides throughout the 1990s.

The relationship between the British Government and the republican movement is central to the Northern Ireland peace process and the search for a solution. As the conflict continued throughout the 1980s, relations between republicans and the British Government were defined by intense suspicion and opposition. Republicans were opposed to Thatcher's handling of the 1981 hunger strikes and the death of ten republican prisoners. For Thatcher's part, she had personal knowledge of IRA atrocities as her friend and colleague Airey Neave, Conservative spokesperson on Northern Ireland was killed by the Irish National Liberation Army (INLA) in 1979 and in 1984 the IRA had tried to kill her and her cabinet colleagues in the Brighton bombing. Despite the British Government's policy marginalisation of Sinn Féin it seemed that republicans had no intention of ending their campaign of violence without British withdrawal. However, by the end of the 1980s and early 1990s there were signs that the Sinn Féin leadership was prepared to reassess republican strategy and the means for attaining a united Ireland. As McGarry and O'Leary point out, republicans recognised that they 'were not winning, militarily or politically'.[10]

The British response to these developments by Sinn Féin was to try to facilitate republican transition away from violence. From the late 1980s it is clear that British Government policy shifted to persuade republicans to abandon the 'armed struggle' and embark on the path of democratic politics. Secretary of State Peter Brooke's statement in November 1990 that Britain had 'no selfish or strategic or economic interest in Northern Ireland' is important here as it appeared to contradict the traditional republican view of Britain's imperial interest in Northern Ireland. In February 1992 Secretary of State for Northern Ireland Patrick Mayhew delivered a speech in which he suggested that following republicans' rejection of violence there would be potential for movement towards inter-party talks on the future of Northern Ireland.

British contacts with the IRA

The shift in policy also involved the opening of secret back-channel contacts with the IRA. In 1990 the British Government embarked on this new policy to persuade republicans to move away from violence as they came to the view that a straightforward defeat of the IRA was not going to be possible and that their approach should be to focus on and facilitate the intriguing noises of change coming from the republican leadership. The series of secret back-channel contacts between the British Government and Sinn Féin representatives continued from October 1990 until late 1993.

Republicans' response to the new approach on the part of the British Government was extremely positive. Hennessey notes that republicans were delighted with Brooke's statement which they interpreted as a sign of British weakness. Significantly, republicans embraced the opportunity to engage with the British Government in the context of the back-channel contacts.[11] In 1991 Gerry Adams stated: 'The Sinn Féin position is that, when you have the conditions for conflict, how you end the conflict is to change the conditions'.[12]

Republicans had been excluded from British Government initiatives such as Sunningdale and at the Brooke–Mayhew talks in 1991–2. Now republicans could take part in constitutional politics as long as they adopted purely democratic means to pursue their goals. Importantly, the British Government displayed a readiness to explore the opportunity to facilitate Sinn Féin's transition. Indeed, it appears that the British Government held the view that to secure a settlement and the end of the conflict, it was necessary for Sinn Féin to be part of the peace process.

As we saw in the previous chapter, the Downing Street Declaration was hugely significant as it opened the door for Sinn Féin to become involved in all-party talks. Although republicans found the text somewhat disappointing, it nevertheless formed part of the background of the IRA move towards its ceasefire in 1994. Meanwhile, the series of back-channel contacts between the British Government and Sinn Féin ended in November 1993. As Hennessey writes, 'The British would not budge from their insistence that there had to be a permanent end to violence and that this had to be demonstrated. The British adherence to the principle of consent and the refusal to become a persuader for Irish unity were fixed principles'.[13] It was clear, however, that the British Government had shifted its policy from exclusion of republicans in the 1970s and 1980s and was now seeking to create a new political landscape whereby Sinn Féin could become engaged in inter-party discussions.

A new political environment was created in the wake of the IRA ceasefire announced in 1994. In March 1995 the British Government suggested that a 'token' act of decommissioning would be sufficient for Sinn Féin to take part in negotiations. However, the IRA broke its ceasefire in February 1996 with the bombing of Canary Wharf in London. Sinn Féin contested the election to the Northern Ireland Forum in 1996, a body set up to advance negotiations, winning seventeen seats. The Labour victory at the 1997 Westminster election and Tony Blair becoming Prime Minister changed the dynamic. Blair announced another round of inter-party talks which provided a major incentive for republicans to move away from violence. With the IRA's statement of its renewed ceasefire in July 1997, the condition of prior decommissioning was abandoned and Sinn Féin entered talks in September.

Republicans have on a number of occasions been highly critical of the British Government's decisions in the aftermath of the 1998 Agreement. For instance, Sinn Féin was vehemently opposed to the Blair administration's moves to suspend the devolved institutions under the Northern Ireland Act 2000 which they viewed as a move to save David Trimble. Significantly, republicans have since accorded the British Government a positive contribution in the search for agreement between the two traditions. This view was expressed by Martin McGuinness who suggested that British Prime Minister Tony Blair made a tremendous contribution to the peace process and that without his commitment and that of Taoiseach Bertie Ahern the process would have collapsed.[14]

The British Government and unionism

The relationship between the British Government and the unionist community in Northern Ireland has been problematic throughout the course of 'the Troubles' and the peace process. On the one hand, unionists looked to London to secure their interests and maintain the Union. However, unionists have also been extremely suspicious of British intentions in Northern Ireland and have often felt a sense of betrayal in relation to British actions which unionists have viewed as appeasement to nationalists and concessions to republicans. Thus, successive British Governments have been caught in a difficult situation. They have been keen to bring Sinn Féin into the process and at the same time reassure unionists that Northern Ireland's constitutional status would not change without majority consent.

It is important to remember that unionists protested against home rule for Ireland in the late nineteenth and early twentieth centuries but then agreed to have a separate parliament at Stormont in Belfast and the creation of Northern Ireland which would remain within the UK. During the Stormont years of unionist control from 1921 to 1972 the Westminster Parliament was at arm's length from developments in Northern Ireland. This situation changed with the outbreak of 'the Troubles' and the collapse of Stormont which was prorogued by the British Government in 1972. Heath's Cabinet came to the view that something radical had to be done, particularly in the wake of Faulkner's disastrous internment policy and the impact of 'Bloody Sunday'. Northern Ireland Prime Minister Brian Faulkner felt that a special relationship existed between his party and the Conservative Government in London under Edward Heath and he expected nothing to change. Faulkner was to be shocked and disappointed, however, at the British Government's decision to take full control of security and legal powers in Northern Ireland. Faulkner's unionists felt betrayed by Heath and resigned as a cabinet.

Relations between the British Government and unionists were also severely strained under Margaret Thatcher's premiership. On one level, Thatcher was wholly committed to the Union and claimed that Northern Ireland was as British as her own constituency. However, this commitment to the Union did not translate into unwavering support for the unionist position. A hugely significant event in the relationship between the British Government and unionism was the signing of the AIA between Thatcher and Taoiseach Garret FitzGerald in 1985. For unionists, the AIA was a huge betrayal. They responded with street protests in opposition to the accord and all fifteen Unionist MPs resigned their Westminster seats, forcing by-elections on the issue in January 1986 (one unionist seat was lost to Seamus Mallon, SDLP). Overall, the British–unionist relationship was seriously strained by the AIA.

A key challenge for successive British Governments from Major to Blair has been the need to reconcile the objective of facilitating republicans while keeping unionists on board. Interestingly, the Ulster Unionists found themselves in a seemingly favourable position at Westminster under the Major administration. As Major's majority in the House of Commons was somewhat eroded the UUP expected to have a considerable influence on government policy. It is true that Major consulted UUP leader James Molyneaux over the contents of the DSD; Thatcher's government had failed to consult unionists over the Anglo-Irish Agreement and Major was keen to avoid a similar reaction. However, it is also arguable that Molyneaux overestimated his party's influence with the Major administration. By the end of 1993 with the DSD both governments had clearly moved to a more inclusive approach seeking to encourage the reappraisal within republicanism and ultimately secure Sinn Féin's participation in the political process.

Blair Government

With the Labour victory at the 1997 Westminster election unionists were fearful that the Blair administration would have pro-nationalist leanings. However, in relation to building positive relations with unionist politicians it was helpful that Blair abandoned his party's traditional policy on Irish unity by consent. That said, the unionist community was not terribly keen on Blair's first Secretary of State for Northern Ireland Mo Mowlam who was considered to have nationalist sympathies (UUP leader Trimble chose to bypass Mowlam and the Northern Ireland Office and dealt almost exclusively with 10 Downing Street).

In the context of the 1998 Agreement, unionists were highly critical of what they viewed as the British Government's concessions to republicans: the release of prisoners; reform of the police including change of name from the RUC to the Police Service of Northern Ireland; and Sinn Féin in government in advance of IRA decommissioning. At the time of the negotiations in April 1998 Trimble obtained a side-letter to the Agreement from Blair which stated that the British Government would support any necessary changes to the Agreement to ensure that parties who failed to fulfil their responsibilities would be excluded and that the process of IRA decommissioning should begin straight away. The letter did not have much impact, however, as the stop–start decommissioning process alienated the unionist community and created huge difficulties for Trimble's leadership. Indeed, Trimble has criticised Blair for going out of his way to ease republican difficulties while failing to address the falling unionist support for the 1998 Agreement.[15]

The Irish Government: the irredentism claim

The Irish Government has also played a key role in the search for finding a solution to the conflict in Northern Ireland. Just as the British state was viewed differently by nationalists and unionists, the Irish state has also been perceived as having diverging motivations on the part of the local parties. On the one hand, nationalists and republicans looked to successive Irish Governments as the guardians of the Irish nation and supporters of the goal of Irish unity in talks with the British government. On the other hand, unionists were opposed to what they saw as the Irish Republic's irredentist claim to Northern Ireland in the Irish Constitution. They also viewed the Irish state as alien and inhospitable, a religiously homogeneous state unwelcome to the unionist, Protestant community.

The 1937 Irish Constitution

In relation to the role of the Irish Republic in the Northern Ireland peace process, it is crucial to consider the contentious claim of the Irish state on the territory of Northern Ireland in Articles Two and Three of the 1937 Irish Constitution:

> Article Two: The national territory consists of the whole island of Ireland, its islands and the territorial seas.
>
> Article Three: Pending the re-integration of the national territory, and without prejudice to the right of Parliament and Government established by this constitution to exercise jurisdiction over the whole of that territory, the laws enacted by that Parliament shall have the like area and extent of application as the laws of Soarstát Éireann and the like extra-territorial effect.

The Irish Constitution, therefore, meant that everyone living on the island of Ireland was considered part of the Irish nation. In other words, Northern Ireland was part of the Irish nation and the Irish state. As highlighted later in the chapter, this territorial claim to Northern Ireland on the part of the Irish Republic was vehemently opposed by unionists. Articles Two and Three were then amended in the context of negotiations leading to the Good Friday/Belfast Agreement of 1998.

There are two main parties in the Republic of Ireland: Fianna Fáil and Fine Gael, both of whom seek the reunification of Ireland. It is interesting that both parties have used their policies on Northern Ireland as a crucial element in electoral competition. As Catherine O'Donnell notes 'In electoral terms Northern Ireland necessitates an intelligible and productive approach so as to assure the electorate of competency and it is at this level that parties compete with one another'.[16] This competition was particularly evident between Fianna Fáil's Charles Haughey and Garret FitzGerald of Fine Gael. In the 1980s little divided the two parties and Haughey adopted republican rhetoric to set Fianna Fáil apart from its electoral rivals.

The inter-party competition was acute when FitzGerald as Taoiseach advocated reform to Articles Two and Three of the Irish Constitution to address unionist concerns. In response, Haughey criticised FitzGerald for compromising on the national question.

How did Irish government policy on Northern Ireland shift over the years?

As a government party for most of the duration of 'the Troubles', Northern Ireland was a key policy area for Fianna Fáil. The party, therefore, needed to adopt a policy which would help to secure a peaceful settlement. This was somewhat challenging given the existence of a republican wing within the party and the resultant unionist suspicions of their intentions. O'Donnell explains the important relationship between Fianna Fáil's policy and ideology: 'The peace process involved reconciling the ideological commitment to unity and the integrity of the nation with a policy and language that gave practical recognition to Northern Ireland, so as to enable the abandonment of anti-partitionist rhetoric'.[17] While Lynch took an anti-partitionist stance and Haughey was known for his doctrinaire nationalism, Albert Reynolds adopted a more pragmatic approach and Bertie Ahern was keen to address unionist concerns.

For both Fianna Fáil and Fine Gael the priority was to try to end republican violence in Northern Ireland. In the 1980s this led to a policy of marginalising republicans, as evidenced by FitzGerald's policy in negotiations with the Thatcher Government leading to the Anglo-Irish Agreement. Similar to the experience of the British Government, Dublin's policy shifted at the end of the 1980s and early 1990s in response to developments within the republican movement, and the policy focused on trying to encourage republicans into mainstream politics.

The relationship between the Irish government and the SDLP was central to this new approach. As Taoiseach from 1992 Albert Reynolds' relationship with John Hume and the SDLP was central to the development of the Irish Government's policy on Northern Ireland. Hennessey suggests that Reynolds moderated the traditional Fianna Fáil policy on Northern Ireland: 'Fianna Fáil was now wedded to Hume's definition of self-determination, which included the consent of the people of Northern Ireland to any change in that

Table 5.2 Irish Prime Ministers (Taoiseach/Taoisigh *pl.*) 1968–2008

Date	Taoiseach	Party
November 1966	Jack Lynch	Fianna Fáil
March 1973	Liam Cosgrave	Fine Gael
July 1977	Jack Lynch	Fianna Fáil
December 1979	Charles Haughey	Fianna Fáil
June 1981	Garret FitzGerald	Fine Gael
March 1982	Charles Haughey	Fianna Fáil
December 1982	Garret FitzGerald	Fine Gael
March 1987	Charles Haughey	Fianna Fáil
February 1992	Albert Reynolds	Fianna Fáil
December 1994	John Bruton	Fine Gael
June 1997–	Bertie Ahern	Fianna Fáil

region's constitutional status; and had retreated from Haughey's position on a unitary state and, apparently previous Irish government positions on joint authority'.[18]

Irish Government policy shifted again following the Fianna Fáil election victory in 1997 with Bertie Ahern becoming Taoiseach. Ahern's premiership displayed a change of approach to the parties in Northern Ireland. The Irish Government would no longer be focused solely on the need to include republicans – the inclusive rather than exclusive policy. Ahern and the Department of Foreign Affairs in Dublin now sought to reach out to all the parties and ensure their continued participation in the peace process. Significantly, this necessitated a greater understanding of unionist identity in Northern Ireland and engagement with unionist politicians. Alongside the Blair administration, the Ahern Government sought to uphold the peace process and the 1998 Agreement as the blueprint for a settlement between the two communities.

The 'pan-nationalist front'

An important factor in the peace process relates to the relationship between the Irish Government and the nationalist and republican politicians in Northern Ireland. An argument exists that the Irish Government along with the SDLP and latterly Sinn Féin represented a 'pan-nationalist' front in the peace process in order to present a common nationalist perspective and negotiating position. O'Donnell notes the origins of the 'pan-nationalist front':

> By the late 1980s Sinn Féin, the SDLP and Fianna Fáil were search-ing for an alternative and broader approach to advance their aims. The strategies of the three parties coincided, since Sinn Féin recog-nized the need for the support of wider nationalist opinion and both the SDLP and Fianna Fáil had come to accept that Sinn Féin must be involved in any future negotiations with the British government and the unionists.[19]

As noted in Chapter 3, an important goal for the SDLP was to promote the 'Irish dimension' as part of any agreed settlement. On becoming party leader, John Hume developed his links with the Irish Government as well as Irish America and the Washington adminis-tration. The New Ireland Forum established by FitzGerald in 1983 was an important demonstration of the developing relations among constitutional nationalist parties. Although invited, unionist parties declined to participate. The Forum published a report in 1984 which put forward three alternative arrangements for a new Ireland: a unitary state; a federal/confederal structure includ-ing Northern Ireland; and joint authority whereby the British and Irish Governments would both have responsibility for the adminis-tration of Northern Ireland. Each of three proposals was rejected by Thatcher (in her 'out, out, out' speech) and by the unionist parties.

The developing relations between the nationalist parties also extended to discussions with Sinn Féin by the end of the 1980s. As noted previously, SDLP leader John Hume embarked on dialogue with Sinn Féin President Gerry Adams in 1988. Although these talks did not come to anything, they re-commenced in the early 1990s and led to the Hume–Adams statement on Irish self-determination in 1993. There were, of course, profound disagreements between the two parties on the role of the British state in the conflict, on the issue of self-determination and the use of violence.[20] Nevertheless, these discussions helped inform the Reynolds Government's drafting of text which led to the DSD of 1993. And just as Hume sought to persuade republicans to abandon their armed campaign, so too did successive Irish Governments see republican violence as the central issue to be tackled.

Discussions with republicans

Discussions also commenced between the Irish Government and republicans in 1988. As O'Donnell points out, it is important to acknowledge the role of Taoiseach Charles Haughey in setting up talks between his adviser Dr Martin Mansergh and Dermot Ahern TD and republicans in 1988.[21] Haughey, therefore, facilitated Sinn Féin's transition away from violence towards constitutional politics, a policy which developed as a central feature of the developing peace process. The 'pan-nationalist front' thus existed as a kind of twin track approach with the Hume–Adams dialogue and Fianna Fáil–Sinn Féin talks. According to O'Donnell, 'The SDLP's involvement was crucial to Northern Ireland politics; the involvement of Fianna Fáil was vital to popular support in the Republic of Ireland and to the building of a wider nationalist consensus which formed the basis of the peace process'.[22]

From 1992 the Reynolds administration coincided with Sinn Féin re-evaluating its strategy and reassessing the armed campaign. There were increasing signals from republican quarters that they wanted to pursue an alternative approach away from violence and to pursue the goal of a united Ireland by purely political means. The pan-nationalist front played a central role in helping facilitate the republican transition. Irish Taoiseach Albert Reynolds, therefore, carried on the contacts that were made with republicans under the Haughey administration. The dialogue cemented under Reynolds became a central element of Dublin's ongoing contribution to the peace process throughout the 1990s. Indeed, the relationship between the Irish Government and Sinn Féin was central to the unfolding peace process from the end of the 1980s and throughout the 1990s leading to the signing of the Good Friday Agreement in 1998.

The Irish Government and unionism

The relationship between the Irish state and the unionist community in Northern Ireland was problematic for a number of reasons. As mentioned above, Articles Two and Three of the Irish Constitution contained a territorial claim to Northern Ireland. This claim was obviously hugely difficult for the British Government and the unionist community. Unionists objected to the fact that the Irish Constitution did not recognise the legal existence of Northern Ireland as part of the UK. Moreover, unionists did not consider themselves to be part of the Irish nation, in contrast to the position of the Irish Constitution that everybody living on the island of Ireland was part of the Irish nation.

To understand the relationship between the Irish state and unionists, it is necessary to appreciate the perception of the Irish state held by unionists. Unionists clearly felt threatened and to an extent under siege from across the border. They looked to the 1937 Constitution and role of the Catholic Church as evidence of Dublin's **irredentist** claims and a foreign, inhospitable society. Moreover, the Irish Government's affinity with the nationalist community in Northern Ireland clearly alienated the unionists and made them suspicious of Dublin's intentions. This was particularly the case in the context of the 'pan-nationalist front' from the early 1990s. Certainly, over the years there was a profound lack of understanding between unionism and the Irish state.

At the outbreak of 'the Troubles' at the end of the 1960s, the anti-partitionist policy of Irish Taoiseach Jack Lynch was particularly abhorrent to the unionist community. In an almost comical illustration of unionist opposition to the Irish Government's interest in Northern Ireland, the DUP's Ian Paisley threw snowballs at Jack Lynch when he paid a visit to Northern Ireland Prime Minister Terence O'Neill in December 1967. Suspicion and anger on the part of unionists towards the Irish state grew following the outbreak of violence in Northern Ireland when the Irish Government took the decision to set up military hospitals at the border. The unionist view that Dublin was seeking to interfere in Northern Ireland was confirmed by Lynch's decision to make the Irish Defence Forces ready for participation in a peace-keeping operation and his Government's recommendation that a United Nations peace-keeping force should be sent to Northern Ireland.

On 13 August 1969, Lynch made a televised speech on the violence in Northern Ireland, stating that:

> The Irish Government can no longer stand by and see innocent people injured and perhaps worse. It is obvious that the RUC is no longer accepted as an impartial police force. Neither would the deployment of British troops be acceptable nor would they be likely to restore peaceful conditions, certainly not in the long term.[23]

Lynch adopted a clear anti-partitionist stance in relation to Northern Ireland. He believed that partition was the cause of the problem in Northern Ireland and was of the view that the British Government should persuade unionists to accept Irish unity. A hugely damaging and controversial development was the arms crisis in 1970, where some members of Lynch's cabinet (Kevin Boland, Neil Blaney and Charles Haughey) allegedly attempted to import weapons for the IRA's use in Northern Ireland. The arms crisis was obviously very alarming to unionists; they felt it proved that they could not trust the Dublin Government who were plotting to send weapons, thereby contributing to violence.

It can be argued that there was little attempt made by successive Irish Governments to understand the concerns of the unionist community in Northern Ireland. Certainly, Haughey's espousal of republican rhetoric and difficulty with the consent principle did little to comfort unionism. Unionists were less suspicious of Haughey's successor Albert Reynolds, who appeared a much more pragmatic politician and displayed no commitment to Haughey's doctrinaire nationalism. However, under FitzGerald's Fine Gael administration there was an attempt to address unionist fears. FitzGerald proposed reform to Articles Two and Three of the Irish Constitution in a conscious effort to reach out to unionism. FitzGerald also endorsed the

British Government's definition of consent which would effectively give the unionist community a veto over unity.[24]

Ahern Government

Relations between the Irish Government and unionists improved in 1997 when Bertie Ahern became Taoiseach. For instance, in a speech in 1995 aimed at Northern Ireland's unionists, Ahern claimed: 'Irish Nationalism has changed. Irredentism is dead. I know of almost no one who believes it is feasible or desirable to attempt to incorporate Northern Ireland into the Republic or into a united Ireland against the will of a majority there, either by force or coercion'.[25] In the context of the negotiations in April 1998 the Ahern administration agreed to changes to the Irish Constitution as part of an overall agreement. Certainly, the Ulster Unionists wanted to see substantial revisions to the Irish Constitution so that the unionist community would be excluded from the Irish nation and state. For their part, the Irish delegation was prepared to drop the territorial claim and amend the description of the island of Ireland as the 'national territory'.

Since the 1998 Agreement relations between the Irish Government and unionism have continued to improve. That said, there were difficult moments such as the call by UUP leader David Trimble in 2002 to hold a referendum on Northern Ireland's constitutional position when he described the Irish Republic as a 'pathetic, sectarian mono-ethnic, mono-cultural state'.[26] Unionists remain opposed to any potential increased involvement of the Irish state in the affairs of Northern Ireland. This was evident in the reaction to the British and Irish Governments' plan for increased cooperation in the absence of agreement between the DUP and Sinn Féin to share power in 2007. Indeed, DUP leader Ian Paisley claimed that he was coerced into sharing power with republicans to avoid an increased role for the Irish Government. However, the potential for a new era of goodwill between the Irish Government and the DUP was signalled with Paisley's meeting with Ahern in Dublin in April 2007. In what appeared an important milestone in the Northern Ireland peace process, Paisley as First Minister (Designate) said that he hoped that 'old suspicions and discords can be buried forever under the prospect of mutual and respectful co-operation'.[27]

British and Irish convergence

An important theme of the peace process during the 1990s was the strong 'partnership' between the British and Irish Governments. Importantly, this positive relationship whereby the two Governments sought to present a united front was certainly not always the case. Indeed, at the outbreak of 'the Troubles' the British Government viewed the Irish Republic as interfering in matters which were not of its concern. However, at crucial points throughout the peace process the two governments adopted a common approach, particularly during the Blair–Ahern administrations.

As noted previously, British–Irish relations with regard to Northern Ireland were far from positive at the time of the outbreak of 'the Troubles' in the 1960s.[28] The Lynch administration's decision to set up field hospitals near the border was rejected by the British Government, which insisted that the situation was an internal issue for the UK. Dublin involvement was seen as unwanted and unnecessary interference. However, British–Irish relations improved as London came to accept that any solution to the conflict would have to include some involvement by the Irish Republic. For instance, a crucial meeting between Taoiseach Charles Haughey and Margaret Thatcher in 1980 led to a series of intergovernmental meetings which became a central facet of the peace process.

In the early 1980s both governments were concerned at the electoral potential of Sinn Féin and adopted a policy of marginalising republicans. Although the New Ireland Forum report of 1984 produced by the FitzGerald Government and other constitutional nationalist parties was dismissed by Thatcher, she nevertheless proceeded with an intergovernmental approach involving negotiations with the Irish Government. These negotiations then led to the signing of the Anglo-Irish Agreement in 1985.

As we have seen, the policy of both governments shifted at the end of the 1980s and early 1990s towards a more inclusive approach. Their position was moving to the view that a settlement would have to include the participation of Sinn Féin and they sought to facilitate republicans' transition towards mainstream politics. The Major and Reynolds Governments were committed to persuading republicans to abandon violence. The two governments adopted a common policy whereby multi-party talks should be held on the future of Northern Ireland and that all parties not involved in violence would be invited to participate.

Without doubt, the partnership between Blair and Ahern was the crucial British–Irish relationship which proved extremely fruitful for the peace process and arrival at a negotiated peace agreement in 1998. With both parties winning power in 1997, their respective electoral victories had an impact on revitalising the inter-party talks. The energy, time and commitment invested by both premiers in the Northern Ireland process over a period of ten years led to the eventual agreement between nationalism and unionism, most significantly between the DUP and Sinn Féin in 2007. In January 1998 the two governments offered their 'Propositions on Heads of Agreement' document as the basis for agreement. They then played a key role in securing agreement between the UUP and SDLP with both Blair and Ahern present at the negotiations in April 1998.

In the period following suspension of the devolved institutions in 2002 the two governments acted as 'guardians' of the 1998 Agreement, stressing that its provisions would form the blueprint for any future agreement. When agreement between the DUP and Sinn Féin was difficult to achieve at the St Andrews talks in Scotland hosted by the two governments, Blair and Ahern threatened the parties with their so-called 'Plan B' should the parties not be prepared to participate in a devolved power-sharing government. This would entail extended London–Dublin cooperation. Commitment to a joint approach was also evident in the financial package proposed in March 2007 with contributions from both governments. Following agreement between the DUP and Sinn Féin on 26 March 2007 that they would share power from 8 May, Blair stated that everything he and his party had done over the previous ten years was in preparation for that moment.[29] Ahern said the agreement had 'the potential to transform the future of this island'.[30]

....

✔ What you should have learnt from reading this chapter

- The British and Irish Governments played a central role in the Northern Ireland peace process.

- The two governments have had different relationships with nationalism and unionism, respectively.

- The relationship between the two governments and republicans was central to the peace process of the 1990s.

Glossary of key terms

Irredentist Term describing the policy of a state to acquire territory that was once part of the country or considered to have been.

Likely examination questions

What was the role of the British and Irish Governments in the search for a solution in Northern Ireland?

What was the relationship between the British Government and republicanism during the Northern Ireland conflict?

Helpful websites

Government of Ireland: http://www.irlgov.ie

10 Downing Street: http://www.number10.gov.uk

Conflict Archive on the Internet: http://www.cain.ulst.ac.uk

Suggestions for further reading

Thomas Hennessey, *The Northern Ireland Peace Process: Ending the Troubles?*, Dublin: Gill and Macmillan, 2000.

Catherine O'Donnell, *Fianna Fáil, Irish Republicanism and the Northern Ireland Troubles 1968–2005*, Dublin: Irish Academic Press, 2007.

CHAPTER 6

Peace Process to Good Friday Agreement

Contents

Overview

The chapter discusses the unfolding peace process of the mid- to late 1990s which led to the signing of the Good Friday Agreement in 1998. It explores the involvement of republicans in the political process for the first time and the difficult issue of IRA decommissioning in the context of all-party talks. The detail of the institutional structure under the Agreement is discussed in Chapter 7. This chapter considers why the Agreement was deemed 'historic' as a potential end to violence and the Northern Ireland conflict. It then discusses the reasons on the part of the political parties who supported the Agreement and those who opposed it. In particular, the chapter highlights why some unionists viewed it as a vehicle to maintain the Union while nationalists and mainstream republicans viewed the arrangements as a transitional stage to a united Ireland.

Key issues to be covered in this chapter

- The transformed political landscape following the IRA ceasefires leading to Sinn Féin's participation in negotiations
- Why the Good Friday Agreement was heralded as significant and a potential end to the Northern Ireland conflict
- Why some parties supported the Agreement: the Trimble camp of the UUP, the SDLP, mainstream republicans and smaller parties
- Why some parties were opposed to the Agreement: the 'antis' within the UUP, the DUP, the UKUP and some republicans

From negotiations to a deal

Chapter 4 outlined the series of political initiatives designed to solve the conflict that were advanced by the British and Irish Governments and local parties from the 1970s to the early 1990s. As we saw, none of these initiatives satisfied both communities and the conflict continued into the 1990s. The situation was to change, however, over the course of the 1990s. Thus, the 1990s were to be the decade of the Northern Ireland 'peace process' which ultimately led to an agreement between the two communities in 1998.

The unfolding peace process of the 1990s developed for a number of reasons, a central one being the transition within republicanism away from violence and towards democratic politics. The IRA and loyalist ceasefires of 1994 brought about a new political landscape in Northern Ireland. The British and Irish Governments were faced with the difficult issue of how to deal with paramilitary weapons and start a process of decommissioning. With Sinn Féin seeking inclusion in the political process, the question was whether decommissioning should be a precondition of entry into talks. As English notes, in 1993 Secretary of State Patrick Mayhew 'had said that the IRA would have to make its guns and explosives available to demonstrate that its war was over' and that 'Gerry Adams had been warned by Fianna Fáil President Albert Reynolds that illegal arms and equipment would have to be dealt with'.[1] Although the two governments seemingly expected the IRA to decommission some weapons following its ceasefire, republicans were not prepared to do so. As English points out: 'Republicans felt . . . that decommissioning should happen at the end of the negotiations rather than the start'.[2]

To make progress on the decommissioning issue, the two governments set up an international commission chaired by former American Senator George Mitchell. The Mitchell Commission published its report in January 1996 and 'concluded that paramilitary organisations would not decommission any arms before the establishment of all-party talks. But it added that some decommissioning should take place during all-party talks, rather than before, as was the British view'.[3] Thus, the Mitchell Report recommended that decommissioning should take place during the inter-party talks and this, then, removed the prerequisite for decommissioning in advance of entry into negotiations.

Importantly, the Report proposed that all participants in multi-party talks should accept a 'commitment and adherence to fundamental principles of democracy and non-violence'.[4] The principles became known as the six Mitchell Principles and recommended that parties affirm their commitment to democratic and exclusively peaceful means of resolving political disputes, to the total disarmament of all paramilitary organisations, to agree that disarmament should be verified by an independent commission, to renounce the use or threat of force to influence negotiations, to agree to abide by terms of an agreement and to urge an end to 'punishment' killings and beatings.[5]

The peace process encountered a major setback in February 1996 when the IRA broke its ceasefire with a bomb at Canary Wharf in London, killing two people and injuring more than a hundred others. The paramilitary organisation was not satisfied with the progress of the peace process in the period since its ceasefire in 1994. The IRA blamed the collapse of its ceasefire on John Major's Government: 'Instead of embracing the peace process, the British Government acted in bad faith, with Mr Major and the unionist leaders squandering the opportunity to resolve the conflict'.[6] The Prime Minister John Major and Taoiseach John Bruton then set the start of a fresh round of negotiations for 10 June 1996 following elections to a negotiating forum held in May.

The British Government continued to call on the IRA to reinstate its ceasefire and on Sinn Féin to sign up to the Mitchell Principles before the party could be included in negotiations. The British Government also legislated for a Northern Ireland Forum for Political Dialogue from which party delegates to negotiations would be drawn. The elections to the Forum took place on 30 May 2006. It was a particularly good election for Sinn Féin who obtained a record vote of 15.47 per cent and seventeen seats. In addition to the UUP, SDLP and DUP other parties included Alliance, the UKUP, PUP with links to the UVF; the UDP with links to the UDA; the Northern Ireland Women's Coalition; and Labour.[7] The Forum lasted until 1998 and its value is questionable as Sinn Féin never took up any of its seventeen seats and the SDLP withdrew in July 1996. Despite Sinn Féin's electoral success the party remained excluded from the negotiations at Stormont due to ongoing IRA violence. Although the party may have endorsed the six principles in May 1996 the IRA refused to do so.[8] On 15 June 1996 an IRA bomb exploded in Manchester injuring over 200 people and causing millions of pounds worth of damage to the city centre.

The Northern Ireland peace process was reinvigorated on 1 May 1997 when the Labour Party won a landslide victory at the UK General Election. Significantly, the British Government accepted the Mitchell Report, which meant that decommissioning was no longer a prerequisite to entry into talks. The Blair Government did, however, want to see Sinn Féin sign up to the Mitchell Principles on rejecting violence and embracing purely democratic means for pursuing their political goals. Tony Blair's first visit outside London after becoming Prime Minister was to Belfast and he had important messages for both communities. He sought to reassure unionists: 'I am committed to Northern Ireland. I am committed to the principle of consent. My agenda is not a united Ireland'.[9] He also pointedly urged republicans to renounce violence and invited Sinn Féin to participate in the talks, subject to an IRA ceasefire and commitment to democratic politics: 'I want the talks process to include Sinn Féin. The opportunity is still there to be taken. If there is an unequivocal ceasefire words and deeds must match and there must be no doubt of a commitment to peaceful methods and the democratic process'.[10]

On 20 July 1997 the IRA declared a resumption of its 1994 ceasefire. The reinstatement of the IRA ceasefire thus triggered the question whether Sinn Féin would be invited to participate in negotiations. The situation was entirely different in the context of the IRA ceasefire. As Hennessey notes, both the British and Irish Governments wanted Sinn Féin to participate in negotiations: 'Without them the talks were a political process but not a Peace Process'.[11] In August 1997 the Independent International Commission on Decommissioning (IICD) was set up with General John de Chastelain appointed as Chairman. Sinn Féin had signed up to the Mitchell Principles and this opened the door to the party's inclusion in negotiations. The inclusion of Sinn Féin in negotiations is thus a central tenet of the Northern Ireland peace process. Adams and McGuinness met Blair for the first time on 13 October. Importantly, however, the inclusion of Sinn Féin in the talks led the DUP and the UKUP to withdraw.

The negotiations between the parties at Stormont continued for a number of months leading up to the publication of a document,

'Propositions of Heads of Agreement' by the British and Irish Governments on 12 January 1998. The document proposed changes to the Irish Constitution and British constitutional legislation. It advanced a number of ideas for multi-party debate and discussion: a Northern Ireland Assembly with executive and legislative power; a North–South Ministerial Council; a British–Irish Intergovernmental Conference; and north–south implementation bodies. The new arrangements would be 'based on commitment to the principle of consent in all its aspects by both the British and Irish governments'.[12] The two governments' document was rejected outright by Sinn Féin. Although the party failed to produce its own proposals for new political structures, leaving much to the SDLP, it viewed the focus on a Northern Ireland Assembly and the consent principle in the 'Heads of Agreement' as pro-unionist.

Despite Sinn Féin's opposition to the document, the 'Heads of Agreement' provided a focus for more detailed negotiations among the parties on what the new political structures would look like. The talks were based on the three strands as per the Brooke–Mayhew talks of 1991–2. Strand One would cover the internal political structures in Northern Ireland, Strand Two would relate to north–south cooperation and Strand Three would cover east–west relations between the UK and the Republic of Ireland. The main negotiations were conducted between the Ulster Unionists, the SDLP and the British and Irish Governments. Sinn Féin had been suspended for a number of weeks in February over continuing IRA violence and the UDP had also been excluded due to violence carried out by the UDA.

As the talks progressed, a difficulty arose over the extent of powers devolved to a new Assembly. In particular, the UUP and the SDLP had different views on the issue of power sharing. The SDLP wanted to see a fully functioning cabinet government established whereas the Ulster Unionists preferred a network of Assembly committees which would be based on proportionality of party electoral strength but a weaker form of power sharing without executive power. In the end, the Ulster Unionists agreed to full executive power sharing under Strand One as a compromise subject to the limitation on the number of north–south bodies in Strand Two. Independent Chairman of the talks, former US Senator George Mitchell set a deadline for agreement by 9 April. On 6 April he presented a draft agreement which

Box 6.1 Key events during the 1990s peace process

Brooke–Mayhew Talks 1991–2
Downing Street Declaration 1993
IRA ceasefire 1994
Loyalist ceasefire October 1994
Framework Documents 1995
Mitchell Commission Report January 1996
IRA bomb at Canary Wharf, London 9 February 1996
Northern Ireland Forum election 30 May 1996
Start of multi-party talks at Stormont 10 June 1996
Labour won UK General Election May 1997
IRA reinstated ceasefire July 1997
Sinn Féin admitted to inter-party talks September 1997
British and Irish Governments' 'Heads of Agreement' document
    January 1998
Good Friday Agreement signed 10 April 1998

was rejected by the UUP but formed the basis of the final text agreed by the parties on 10 April.

The Good Friday Agreement: an 'historic' deal

The inter-party talks eventually led to the signing of a deal between the parties at Stormont on Good Friday, 10 April 1998. Much has been written about the significance of the Agreement which promised a new era for Northern Ireland through new structures of devolved government and an end to the conflict. While there had been a number of previous political initiatives in the course of the thirty years of the conflict – the Sunningdale Agreement of 1974, the Anglo-Irish Agreement of 1985, the Brooke–Mayhew talks of 1991–2, the Downing Street Declaration of 1993 and the Framework Documents of 1995 – they had all failed to command support from both communities.

As mentioned above, the Agreement contained three separate strands, a format which can be traced back to the Brooke–Mayhew talks of 1991–2. Strand One set out the internal structures for the Assembly and the Executive, Strand Two related to north–south bodies and the North–South Ministerial Council and Strand Three provided for a British–Irish Council. Following referenda in Northern Ireland and the Republic of Ireland and an election to the new Northern Ireland Assembly, a power-sharing Executive would be formed including ministers from the main parties subject to their electoral strength in the Assembly.

The Agreement signed by the parties at Stormont was the culmination of several years of negotiations and a long list of political initiatives stretching back to the 1970s. As Ruane and Todd note, the Agreement was a 'momentous occasion' which seemed to be 'a compromise not simply between unionism and nationalism but between loyalism and republicanism, and promising a permanent cessation of violence'.[13] They highlight, however, that this 'compromise' was only made possible because it was able to accommodate divergent interpretations: many unionists, in particular UUP leader David Trimble, saw it as cementing the Union, while many nationalists and mainstream republicans saw it as a move towards a united Ireland.

Following the signing of the Agreement by the political parties, it was to be approved by the electorate at referenda in Northern Ireland and the Republic of Ireland. A highly visible referendum campaign was organised by those campaigning for a 'Yes' and 'No' vote, respectively. Importantly, the DUP's campaign for a 'No' vote was joined by three UUP members (Willie Ross, William Thompson and Roy Beggs) as well as the UKUP. In terms of the 'Yes' camp, Tony Blair travelled to Northern Ireland to campaign for a positive result. Speaking to the Royal Agricultural Society in Belfast, Blair said: 'You will all make up your own minds about the agreement. It is your decision. But I honestly believe that to say Yes is to say yes to hope, to peace, to stability, and to prosperity. A No vote is to turn your back on the future'.[14] There were a number of events designed to encourage people to vote 'Yes'. For instance, UUP leader David Trimble and SDLP leader John Hume appeared together on stage with Bono from U2 at a concert at the Waterfront Hall in Belfast.

The referenda and Assembly election

At the referenda on 22 May 1998 the Agreement was approved by a large majority in Northern Ireland (71 per cent) on a record turnout of 81 per cent in a domestic UK jurisdiction and an overwhelming majority in the South (94 per cent) on an average turnout of 56 per cent. It is important to note, however, that a substantial number of unionists rejected it; an RTE/Lansdowne exit poll reported that 55 per cent of those who described themselves as unionist supported the Agreement at the Northern Ireland referendum. The referendum in the Republic of Ireland included changes to the Irish Constitution in relation to the reform of Articles Two and Three.

The referenda then paved the way for the June 1998 Assembly elections with the results rather more of a mixed bag. Out of the 108 Assembly members forty-two nationalists (twenty-four seats for the SDLP and eighteen for Sinn Féin) and eight 'others' (six from the Alliance Party and two from the Women's Coalition) were willing to support the Agreement. The fifty-eight unionists, however, were narrowly divided. Thirty MLAs were members of parties which endorsed the Agreement – UUP (twenty-eight seats) and PUP (two seats) – while twenty-eight unionist MLAs were from parties which rejected it – DUP (twenty seats), UKUP (five seats) and dissident Ulster Unionists (three seats). This meant that there was a clear nationalist majority in favour of the Agreement and thirty unionists supported the deal, just narrowly ahead of the twenty-eight unionists who opposed it.

Why was the Good Friday Agreement significant?
As noted above, the Good Friday Agreement was highly significant as it was an agreement between the two communities and included Sinn Féin as well as the loyalist parties. With republicans signing up to the deal it meant an end to IRA violence and promised a new, peaceful era for Northern Ireland. The Agreement was also significant as its institutional structure created not just new internal arrangements for devolved power sharing, but also institutions to reflect the links with both the Republic of Ireland and with Britain.

The academic literature on the Agreement points to a number of reasons why the deal was significant. For instance, Paul Arthur maintains that the significance of the Agreement in comparison with previous initiatives, in particular Sunningdale, is in its creative management of identity. The people of Northern Ireland can now identify and be accepted as Irish or British or *both* and MLAs are to designate themselves as unionist, nationalist or *other*. Arthur contends that this approach was 'the culmination of a movement away from exclusion and polycentric identities and a blurring of boundaries'.[15] Respect for identity is central to the ethos of the Agreement. As O'Leary writes, this respect for the two identities in Northern Ireland leads to a 'double protection model' which:

> promises protection to Northern nationalists now on the same terms that will be given to Ulster unionists should they ever become a minority in a united Ireland. Communities are to be protected whether they are majorities or minorities, and whether sovereignty lies with the United Kingdom or the Republic, hence, the expression double protection.[16]

We have already noted the significance of the Agreement in that it included the participation of republicans in contrast to previous initiatives. This is noted by Horowitz who develops the contrast with previous attempts as the Agreement offered the republican movement the opportunity to become involved in the political process for the first time. Horowitz notes that 'Previous attempts at conciliation, most notably the "power-sharing government" of 1973–4, had been premised on the assumption that moderate unionists and moderate nationalists should join together against those who were unwilling to co-operate with the other side'.[17] This was not to be the case with the rolling peace process of the 1990s which culminated in the signing of the Agreement. Horowitz explains that what transpired was a realisation on the part of the political parties of the 'main "lesson" of history: so many efforts had failed to produce a politics of intergroup accommodation that it was time for a bold new departure. An inclusive regime, with air-tight minority guarantees, had not yet been tried'.[18]

The Good Friday Agreement was clearly significant for a number of reasons. The negotiations and signing of the deal had included Sinn Féin and promised an end to paramilitary violence. The inclusion of republicans meant that republicans would for the first time take seats in a parliament and government at Stormont. The text of the Agreement provided for the respect of both traditions as people could identify as British or Irish or both. The Agreement established new institutional structures to reflect both north–south and east–west relations, and it included the reform of Articles Two and Three of the Irish Constitution.

Support for the Agreement

A key feature of the Agreement was that it had something for both unionists and nationalists who were prepared to support it. Thus, it is important to consider that the parties supported the deal for very different reasons. Moreover, it is crucial to understand that there was some divergence in interpretation of what the Agreement meant *within* as well as between the unionist community and the wider republican movement. In other words, there were significant divisions within Ulster Unionism and within republicanism over what the Agreement would mean for Northern Ireland's present and future constitutional status.

The Agreement was supported by the UUP (although a section of the party was sceptical), the SDLP, Sinn Féin, the Alliance Party, the Women's Coalition and the two loyalists parties: the PUP and the UDP. Importantly, there were divisions within the UUP over whether the Agreement would finally settle the issue of Northern Ireland's constitutional status. The pro-Agreement camp within the UUP was led by party leader David Trimble. From Trimble's perspective, the Agreement was 'as good and as fair as it gets'.[19] Of particular importance for unionists was the reform to Articles Two and Three of the Irish Constitution.

For Trimble, it was crucial to be involved in determining the substance of any new deal. While his intra-communal rivals in the DUP and UKUP had not taken part in the talks due to Sinn Féin's inclusion, the UUP was of the view that it was politically necessary for them to take an important role in the negotiations. As Aughey points out, it had seemed to unionists that it was nationalists and republicans who had been making gains, particularly since the Anglo-Irish Agreement: 'The convincing moral was that unionists should become active participants in, rather than a passive victim of, political change'; with David Trimble becoming leader of the UUP in 1995 he 'promised to replace the "do nothing" style of Unionist leadership'.[20] For Trimble, then, it was necessary to remain involved in the talks, particularly since the other unionist parties offered no alternative. Trimble pointed to the reform of Articles Two and Three of the Irish Constitution as evidence that support for the Agreement secured important long-term unionist objectives. The UUP leader also sought to secure the decommissioning of IRA weapons in return for Sinn Féin's inclusion in the new Executive, hence his 'guns for government' stance. As we will see in the next chapter, the issue of decommissioning became highly controversial and problematic for the new administration.

The 1998 Agreement was also supported by loyalist parties and paramilitary organisations. The PUP campaigned for a 'Yes' vote in the referendum and then won two seats at the June Assembly election. The PUP had wanted for some time to see new political structures agreed which would maintain Northern Ireland's place within the UK. Indeed, it appears that an important contribution was made by the PUP and the UDP who provided a level of support for Trimble's position within the wider unionist and loyalist communities. On 24 April 1998 the UDA issued a statement in support of the Agreement; their view was that the deal cemented Northern Ireland's place within the UK and that it would not lead to a united Ireland. A statement issued on 15 May 1998 on behalf of the Loyalist Volunteer Force (LVF), however, encouraged people to vote 'No' 'to remain British and hold on to everything Protestant people hold dear'.[21]

With regard to republicanism, Sinn Féin had participated in the talks but had less of an input into the terms of the Agreement than the SDLP and UUP. Indeed, the party was quite slow in confirming its support for the final deal. A crucial issue for Sinn Féin was whether it would take up its Assembly seats at Stormont following the June 1998 election. To decide on the matter the party held a specially convened *ard fheis* on the Agreement on 10 May where its policy to take seats in the Assembly was overwhelmingly endorsed by delegates. The *ard fheis* was attended by a number of IRA prisoners known as the Balcombe Street gang, who had recently been released by the Irish Government as a confidence-building measure. While the attendance by the former prisoners and their support for the Agreement encouraged republicans to support the deal, the televised image of them receiving a hero's reception at the *ard fheis* was difficult for many unionists. The Sinn Féin leadership argued that the Agreement weakened the Union and that a united Ireland would come about in the future with a majority in the north secured by demographic change. Thus, republicans saw the new structures as a transitional phase; they pointed to the north–south bodies as evidence of all-Ireland logic and supported the release of all prisoners within two years.

It is clear, then, that the Sinn Féin leadership believed that while a united Ireland was not yet attainable in the context of the Agreement, it remained the future prize. As Sinn Féin leader Gerry Adams writes of the Agreement in his memoirs:

> Our view was that it was transitional . . . We knew from the parameters of the talks laid down by the two governments that Irish unity would not come out of this phase of the negotiations, but we set ourselves the task of weakening the British link while defending Irish national rights.[22]

At the multi-party talks Sinn Féin had focused on issues such as prisoner releases, policing and equality, leaving the detail of Strand One to the SDLP and UUP. As outlined below, however, there was a section of republicans who were opposed to the Agreement and the prospect of Sinn Féin ministers in a Stormont government.

The terms of the Agreement were held as a victory for the SDLP as they included aspects of policy advocated by the party since the start of 'the Troubles'. Thus, it can be said that the SDLP had a greater sense of ownership of the Agreement than any other party. Indeed, the SDLP had a considerable input into the drafting of the text and negotiating its terms with the UUP. Of particular relevance, of course, was the presence of the 'Irish dimension' as expressed by the North–South Ministerial Council and north–south cooperation bodies in Strand Two of the Agreement. In addition, the SDLP had long proposed new political structures in Northern Ireland based on executive power sharing between the unionist and nationalist parties. As Murray and Tonge note, 'The nationalist elements built into the Good Friday Agreement echoed elements of SDLP political strategy contained in unpublished internal documents dated September 1971'.[23] In relation to the question of whether the Agreement was a final settlement to the Northern Ireland conflict, it is noted that 'the SDLP was ambiguous over the extent to which the Good Friday Agreement ought to represent a final settlement, or a staging post to Irish unity'.[24]

The Agreement was also supported by the Alliance Party and the Northern Ireland Women's Coalition (NIWC). With two candidates elected to the Northern Ireland Forum in 1996 the NIWC made an important contribution to the talks which culminated with the Agreement in 1998. The party then had two candidates elected to the Northern Ireland Assembly at the June election. Both parties celebrated the signing of the Agreement as the beginning of a new era in Northern Ireland and cooperation between the two communities. Alliance and the NIWC campaigned for a 'Yes' vote in the referendum. Alliance won six Assembly seats in June 1998 with one of its MLAs, Lord Alderdice becoming Speaker of the new Assembly.

Opposition to the Agreement

A hugely important feature of Northern Ireland politics following the signing of the Good Friday Agreement was the extent of the division within the unionist community over the deal. Although the UUP was a key participant in the negotiations and the party leader sought to persuade the unionist community of the merits of the Agreement, there were sceptics within the party who did not share Trimble's view. The Ulster Unionist Assembly Party included three independent unionists who were extremely sceptical about the Agreement. Moreover, Ulster Unionist MP Jeffrey Donaldson had left the talks over the decommissioning issue and announced he would vote 'No' in the referendum on the Agreement.

The anti-Agreement unionist position was represented by the DUP and the UKUP. For these two parties, the Agreement could mean only a slippery slope towards a united Ireland. The anti-Agreement position of the DUP involved strong criticism of the UUP under David Trimble's leadership. At the DUP annual conference on 28 November 1998 Peter Robinson said:

> The Ulster Unionist Party under Trimble's leadership is the party of broken promises and shattered pledges. They are the party, without whose support Provisional IRA men would never have been released from prison, and without whom, the RUC would not presently be waiting to hear the form of its destruction. They are the Party who provided places in Government for terrorist front-men and who agreed to set up unaccountable all-Ireland Executive bodies – the embryo of a united Ireland.[25]

Both the DUP and the UKUP, led by Robert McCartney, were opposed to the inclusion of Sinn Féin in a power-sharing executive. Unionists opposed to the Agreement launched a joint campaign, 'It's Right to Say No'. The UKUP won five seats at the June Assembly election, although four MLAs later left the party and formed the Northern Ireland Unionist Party, leaving McCartney as the sole MLA for the UKUP. The anti-Agreement unionists argued that the Agreement would allow terrorists to enter government and sought to encourage people to vote 'No' in the referendum. The parties stated that they would contest the election and successful candidates would take their Assembly seats but would continue to oppose the Agreement and the inclusion of republicans. McCartney believed that the Agreement would lead to a change in the constitutional status of Northern Ireland leading to a united Ireland. In a newspaper article he stated that he believed decommissioning would not occur until Sinn Féin realised its objective of Irish unity.[26] The DUP and UKUP were also opposed to the early release of paramilitary prisoners, the extent of north–south cooperation and the reform of the RUC. In May 1998 the Orange Order also called on its members to vote 'No' in the referendum.

While there was an important divergence of interpretation of the Agreement on the part of unionists, there was a significant rift within republicanism on whether the Agreement was the best course of action to bring about the goal of a united Ireland. Republican Sinn Féin was opposed to the Agreement and the 'Real IRA' issued a statement saying that a military campaign would resume. The latter group was responsible for the Omagh bomb of August 1998 in opposition to Sinn Féin's support for the Agreement, which they viewed as a betrayal of the goal of a united Irish republic. Other anti-Agreement republican positions held that the Agreement was partitionist and guaranteed Northern Ireland's constitutional status quo. They vehemently opposed the idea that Sinn Féin members would take seats in a government at Stormont. Republican commentator Anthony McIntyre argued that by entering the Assembly 'republicans are included minus republicanism. The republican argument becomes marginalised anyway. Consequently, the British state will have rendered ineffectual the most potent challenge its rule has faced in Ireland since partition'.[27]

Table 6.1   Parties' support for/opposition to the Agreement

Party	Position	Reasons
SDLP	Supported	Internal power sharing between the two communities; increased north–south cooperation; North–South Ministerial Council
Sinn Féin	Supported	Viewed Agreement as transitional phase towards Irish unity; increased north–south cooperation
UUP	Supported (but some opposed)	Viewed Agreement as cementing NI's position in the UK; reform of Irish Constitution's Articles 2 and 3; internal devolved structures; institutions to strengthen east–west relations; British–Irish Council
PUP and UDP	Supported	Viewed Agreement as cementing NI's position in the UK; reform of Irish Constitution's Articles 2 and 3; internal devolved structures; institutions to strengthen east–west relations;

Table 6.1 (cont.)

Party	Position	Reasons
		British–Irish Council; release of paramilitary prisoners
Alliance	Supported	Viewed the Agreement as an opportunity for a new, peaceful and fairer society; devolved power sharing; north–south and east–west structures
NIWC	Supported	Viewed the Agreement as an opportunity for a new peaceful and fairer society; devolved power sharing; north–south and east–west structures
DUP	Opposed	Argued that the Agreement would lead to a united Ireland; inclusion of Sinn Féin in government; north–south cooperation; prisoner releases; reform of the RUC
UKUP	Opposed	Argued that the Agreement would lead to a united Ireland; inclusion of Sinn Féin

Table 6.1 (cont.)

Party	Position	Reasons
		in government; north–south cooperation; prisoner releases; reform of the RUC
Republican Sinn Féin and others such as the 'Real IRA'	Opposed	Viewed the Agreement as a 'partitionist' settlement as it did not change the north's constitutional status; Sinn Féin taking Assembly and Executive seats at Stormont

 What you should have learnt from reading this chapter

- The IRA and loyalist ceasefires of 1994 transformed the political landscape in Northern Ireland. The IRA's reinstated ceasefire in 1997 led to the inclusion of Sinn Féin in talks. The inclusion of republicans was central to the peace process.

- The Good Friday Agreement was significant for a number of reasons: support from unionists, nationalists, loyalists and republicans; new arrangements for devolved power sharing; new institutions to reflect north–south and east–west relations; potential end to paramilitary violence.

- The Agreement was supported by parties for different reasons: the Trimble camp within the UUP and the loyalist parties viewed the Agreement as cementing the Union; the SDLP and Sinn Féin looked to the increased north–south dimension and the institutions as a transitional phase to a united Ireland.

- The Agreement was opposed by the DUP and the UKUP who believed that it would lead to a united Ireland. They were vehemently opposed to the inclusion of Sinn Féin in government prior to IRA decommissioning and were suspicious of the north–south bodies and the North–South Ministerial Council.

- Some republicans opposed the deal as they believed it to be 'partitionist'.

Likely examination questions

Why was the Good Friday/Belfast Agreement of 1998 significant?

Why did some parties support and others oppose the Good Friday/Belfast Agreement of 1998?

Helpful websites

Conflict Archive on the Internet: http://www.cain.ulst.ac.uk

Suggestions for further reading

Thomas Hennessey, *The Northern Ireland Peace Process: Ending the Troubles?*, Dublin: Gill and Macmillan, 2000.

Gerard Murray and Jonathan Tonge, *Sinn Féin and the SDLP: From Alienation to Participation*. Dublin: O'Brien Press, 2005.

Joseph Ruane and Jennifer Todd (eds), *After the Good Friday Agreement: Analysing Political Change in Northern Ireland*, Dublin: University College Dublin Press, 1999.

Rick Wilford (ed.), *Aspects of the Belfast Agreement*, Oxford: Oxford University Press, 2001.

CHAPTER 7

Institutional Framework of the Agreement

Contents

Overview

The Good Friday Agreement established a new set of political institutions in Northern Ireland. This chapter takes a detailed look at these institutions and their operation until the administration's fourth and final suspension in October 2002. The operation of each of the three strands during devolution is evaluated with an assessment of the respective achievements and limitations. The chapter discusses the major difficulties experienced during devolution from 1999 to 2002. The issue of decommissioning is explored as it proved a major obstacle to the full implementation of the Agreement. The chapter also considers the contentious issue of police reform.

Key issues to be covered in this chapter

- Overview of the institutional structures of the three Strands of the Good Friday Agreement
- The successes of the Northern Ireland Assembly and Committee system
- The difficulties encountered by the Northern Ireland Executive
- The operation of Strands Two and Three
- The stalemate over decommissioning as a constant threat to stability of the power-sharing administration
- The issue of police reform where unionists resisted change and nationalists/republicans sought a transformation of the RUC

Strand One: the Northern Ireland Assembly

Powers and procedures of the Northern Ireland Assembly

The Northern Ireland Act 1998 laid down the legislative powers of the Northern Ireland Assembly which would have full legislative and executive authority over policy areas not under the control of Westminster. The Act lists a number of 'excepted' and 'reserved' matters retained by London. 'Excepted' matters apply to policy areas retained by Westminster indefinitely such as international relations, defence, currency and immigration. 'Reserved' matters may be transferred to the Assembly in the future and include policing and criminal law.

Under the Northern Ireland Act 1998 the Assembly has the power to legislate on a range of 'transferred' matters previously under the control of the six direct rule departments. This means the Assembly has control of policy in relation to health, education, trade, environment, transport, agriculture and planning. It is important to note that the Assembly does not have the power to raise taxes. Moreover, the Secretary of State for Northern Ireland remained responsible for policing, security, the criminal justice system and prisons.

The 108 Members of the Legislative Assembly (MLAs) are elected via the **single transferable vote (STV)**, a proportional representation electoral system. Six MLAs are returned in each of the eighteen Northern Ireland constituencies. It was hoped that the use of STV for Assembly elections would lead voters to transfer their vote across the nationalist and unionist blocs. The results of the June 1998 Assembly election, however, show that cross-communal transfers were low. It appears that the vote transfers in 1998 largely took place within the nationalist and unionist blocs and from pro-Agreement communal parties to bi-communal parties such as Alliance and the NIWC rather than across blocs.

It is important to consider that the design of the Assembly acknowledges the communal divisions in Northern Ireland. For example, before taking their Assembly seats the MLAs designate themselves as 'unionist' 'nationalist' or 'other'. The communal designation of MLAs has a practical purpose when it comes to voting in the Assembly. On important issues there is a requirement for a specified level of support from both unionist and nationalist MLAs. Importantly, there has been some criticism of communal designation by those who maintain that it institutionalises sectarianism. The Alliance Party has been particularly vocal in this respect as the party claims that in important votes the view of MLAs designated as 'other' carries less weight than 'nationalist' and 'unionist' MLAs.

Although the Assembly voting procedures outlined in the Agreement provide for some simple majority voting, there are some instances which require **cross-community voting**. The cross-community requirement is confined to 'key' decisions, some of which are set out in the Agreement or determined by a petition of concern on an issue from at least thirty MLAs. Cross-community voting is applied using one of two alternative voting procedures. First, 'parallel consent' requires a majority of MLAs present and voting, including a majority of designated unionists and designated nationalists. Secondly, 'weighted majority' requires 60 per cent of MLAs present and voting, including at least 40 per cent of designated unionists and designated nationalists.

Northern Ireland's communal divisions are also recognised in the posts of First Minister and Deputy First Minister. Under the Agreement the joint premiers would have equal status and were to be elected by the Assembly voting on a cross-community basis. The Agreement specified that the vote had to take place via the 'parallel consent' procedure. The election of David Trimble (UUP) and Seamus Mallon (SDLP) as First Minister and Deputy First Minister, respectively, took place at the inaugural meeting of the Assembly on 1 July 1998. Although the First Minister and Deputy First Minister were agreed at this time, there was a considerable delay in the transfer of power which took place on 2 December 1999 (see below). It is also important to note that the First Minister and Deputy First Minister were the only ministers elected into office by the Assembly following the June 1998 Assembly election. The other ten ministers were nominated by their respective parties under the **d'Hondt** procedure. Chapter 8 will highlight some important revisions to the Northern Ireland Act 1998 under the Northern Ireland (St Andrews Agreement) Act 2006 which provides for a nomination of the First Minister and Deputy First Minister without a cross-community vote in the Assembly.

How successful was the Assembly?

In making an assessment of the Northern Ireland Assembly which operated (albeit with several suspensions) until October 2002, it is important to consider the pro- and anti-Agreement arithmetic in the Assembly. The unionists were narrowly divided between pro- and anti-Agreement camps. Thirty unionist MLAs supported the Agreement (twenty-eight UUP and two PUP), just ahead of the twenty-eight unionists who opposed it (twenty DUP, five UKUP and three dissident Ulster Unionists). Moreover, the DUP was strongly critical of the UUP and this proved a particular challenge for Ulster Unionist leader David Trimble. The Ulster Unionists suffered some losses from their Assembly team following the failure to re-elect Trimble as First Minister in November 2001. In addition to external criticism, Trimble met considerable criticism from within his own party and two of his Assembly colleagues (Peter Weir and Pauline Armitage) opposed his re-election. Weir was expelled from the party and later defected to the DUP; Armitage was suspended from the UUP and later left the party in June 2003.

The vote on Trimble's re-election as First Minister in November 2001, along with Mark Durkan (SDLP) as Deputy First Minister failed due to insufficient unionist support on the cross-community vote. To resolve the impasse three Alliance members and two MLAs from the NIWC re-designated from 'other' to 'unionist' and secured the necessary cross-community vote. The episode raised the issue of whether the communal designation of MLAs was the most appropriate method of securing support from a wide section of the Assembly. Certainly, the Alliance Party was of the view that the episode demonstrated the sectarian nature of the voting system. It is important to note here that the communal designation system was amended by the Northern Ireland (St Andrews Agreement) Act 2006 whereby MLAs cannot change their designation in the course of a term of office except in the situation where they change membership of a political party.

There were some inter-party difficulties visible on the floor of the Assembly over the period. In particular, the anti-Agreement DUP tried to exclude Sinn Féin on a number of occasions, when it employed the petition of concern to trigger Sinn Féin's exclusion but was unable to get the necessary cross-community vote. The Assembly of 1999–2002 worked fairly well, however, despite the inter-party tensions and the difficulties over decommissioning. For instance, during this period of devolution the Assembly produced thirty-six Acts on transferred matters, and at the time of suspension in October 2002 a total of twenty-two Bills in process by the Assembly were reintroduced as Orders in Council at Westminster.[1] As outlined below, an important success of the Assembly was evident in the committee system.

The developing role of Assembly committees

An interesting feature of the Northern Ireland Assembly established by the Good Friday Agreement was the developing role of the Assembly committees. Under the Agreement the committees have an extensive remit. They are able to scrutinise the work of their associated departments, undertake the committee stage of primary legislation, examine secondary legislation, draft inquiry reports and initiate Bills. Thus, the statutory committees enjoyed considerable authority as they are charged by the Agreement to 'advise and assist' the departments 'in the formulation of policy'.

The Assembly established a number of statutory committees to scrutinise the work of their associated departments. There were also a number of standing committees such as the Committee of the Centre, the Business Committee, the Public Accounts Committee, the Audit Committee and the Committee on Procedures. In addition, a number of *ad hoc* committees were set up to deal with particular issues. Under the Agreement the committee chairs and deputy chairs were from different parties to that of the minister. As per the nomination of ministers, committee chairs and deputy chairs are nominated by the parties under the d'Hondt procedure in proportion to their strength in the Assembly. The remaining membership of the committees also adhered to the general proportionality of the parties' respective electoral support.

Significantly, the Assembly committees were largely successful in carrying out their responsibilities. As Tonge notes, 'Away from the grandstanding of the Assembly floor, business was conducted amicably among all the parties'.[2] There was also a notable willingness on the part of the Assembly committees to cooperate with one another. For instance, liaison took place between the Education Committee and the Committee of the Centre over the children's commissioner, between the Education Committee and the Health Committee on the issue of teenage pregnancy and between the Finance Committee and the Enterprise, Trade and Investment Committee on the relief package for business affected by the foot and mouth crisis. In addition to the degree of cooperation between the committees, there was also a good degree of liaison between committees and departments. Although the relationship between committees and departments was good in most cases, the Health Committee had a fairly difficult relationship with the Minister, Bairbre de Brún (Sinn Féin), particularly in relation to the row over the site of Belfast's maternity services.

It can be argued that the committees took on an 'opposition' role in their work of scrutinising the departments. This is significant in relation to the singular power-sharing arrangements in Northern Ireland wherein the parties are guaranteed ministerial seats subject to their strength in the Assembly (see below). When the Executive was formed on 29 November 1999 it included the four main parties: the UUP; the SDLP; the DUP; and Sinn Féin. This left a small opposition in the Assembly as ninety-two out of 108 MLAs belonged to a governing party; a parliamentary opposition role was thus left to the small parties (Alliance and the NIWC) and the committees. The membership of the committees, however, was dominated by MLAs from governing parties. The committees also developed their role in relation to initiating primary legislation. Just before suspension in October 2002 the first committee Bill was tabled by the Standards and Privileges Committee to create an Assembly Commissioner for Standards under the Assembly Ombudsman for Northern Ireland (Assembly Standards) Bill.

The Northern Ireland Assembly established by the Good Friday Agreement and the Northern Ireland Act 1998 was hugely significant as it restored devolution to the region following decades of conflict and failed political initiatives. In terms of an assessment it appears that the Assembly can be considered a success as both pro- and anti-Agreement parties took their seats and debated policy issues at Stormont. It can be argued that the Assembly was fairly efficient in scrutinising and passing legislation and was particularly successful at the level of committees. Indeed, the committees had begun to develop their important role which, arguably, would have been cemented had the administration continued. There were, however, a number of stumbling blocks which contributed to the challenges faced by the Assembly. As discussed below, the issue of paramilitary decommissioning was never very far away and created problems for the four-party coalition. The Assembly also operated against the backdrop of decreasing support from among the unionist community. Furthermore, as the Assembly included elected representatives (and also government ministers on the part of the DUP) who were opposed to the system, it is perhaps not surprising that the Assembly encountered considerable difficulties.

Strand One: the Executive

The four-party coalition formed on 29 November 1999 was the first power-sharing government in Northern Ireland since the short-lived Sunningdale Executive of 1973–4. Significantly, the Executive was comprised of the four main parties, including the anti-Agreement DUP and Sinn Féin. Of particular note are the institutional rules for power sharing under the 1998 Agreement. While the two joint premiers, the First Minister and Deputy First Minister, were elected via a legitimising vote in the Assembly, the other ten ministers were nominated to the departments under the d'Hondt procedure. In short, parties were allocated ministerial positions in proportion to their electoral strength in the Assembly. On the basis of the June 1998 Assembly election the ten portfolios were allocated as follows: UUP three seats; SDLP three seats; DUP and Sinn Féin on two seats.

A consociational institution

As outlined in Chapter 1, consociational theory advances a number of principles for engineering democracy in post-conflict societies. First developed by Dutch political scientist, Arend Lijphart, the main principle of consociationalism is the 'grand coalition' where all the main segments in society are represented in a power-sharing government. The other three principles of consociational theory are proportionality of important posts, segmental autonomy where each communal bloc controls their own affairs and mutual veto. There has been much academic debate on whether consociationalism is the most appropriate approach for designing democratic institutions in deeply divided societies.

Much of the academic literature agrees that the Northern Ireland Executive established by the 1998 Agreement corresponds to a consociational 'grand coalition' as it included representatives from the unionist, nationalist and republican communities. As Lijphart writes, 'The

Table 7.1 Ministers and departments 1999–2002

	Party	Portfolio	Minister
1.	UUP	Enterprise, Trade and Investment	Reg Empey
2.	SDLP	Finance and Personnel	Mark Durkan Durkan became Deputy First Minister in November 2001 and was replaced by Seán Farren
3.	DUP	Regional Development (seat rotated with Gregory Campbell July 2000 to September 2001)	Peter Robinson
4.	Sinn Féin	Education	Martin McGuinness
5.	UUP	Environment	Sam Foster
6.	SDLP	Higher and Further Education, Training and Employment Later changed to Employment and Learning	Seán Farren When Farren took over the Finance and Personnel portfolio, party colleague Carmel Hanna became Minister for Employment and Learning
7.	DUP	Social Development (seat rotated with Maurice Morrow, October 2000 to November 2001)	Nigel Dodds
8.	UUP	Culture, Arts and Leisure	Michael McGimpsey
9.	Sinn Féin	Health, Social Services and Public Safety	Bairbre de Brún
10.	SDLP	Agriculture and Rural Development	Bríd Rodgers

primary characteristic of consociational democracy is that the political leaders of all significant segments of the plural society cooperate in a grand coalition to govern the country'.[3] The Executive also corresponded to the consociational principle of proportionality as the government is formed according to the d'Hondt mechanism. For Lijphart, 'proportionality adds a refinement to the grand coalition concept: not only should all significant segments be represented in decision-making organs, but they should also be represented proportionally'.[4]

It is important to consider briefly the debate on whether the fully inclusive executive formed under d'Hondt is the most appropriate model for power sharing in Northern Ireland. On the one hand, some parties, such as Sinn Féin and the SDLP, believed that a fully inclusive government in which parties are guaranteed ministerial seats was the best way to form a coalition in Northern Ireland. On the other hand, some parties, such as Alliance and the DUP argued that a 'voluntary' coalition would be better where coalition formation would be the result of bargaining between parties following an election.

Under the alternative arrangement the actual configuration of the coalition would be subject to inter-party negotiations and a legitimising vote requiring sufficient support in the Assembly. Thus, parties would negotiate over which parties should form a government, who should get which portfolios and the content of the new government's policy platform. At the time of writing it is questionable whether the SDLP, and certainly Sinn Féin, would support this alternative to fully inclusive power sharing under d'Hondt. One should not rule out, however, the possibility of further changes to the Agreement in the future.

The delay to executive formation

The new power-sharing government was formed after a considerable delay following the signing of the Good Friday Agreement on 10 April 1998. Although the Assembly election was held in June 1998 and the inaugural meeting of the shadow Assembly took place on 1 July 1998, power was not devolved to the new institutions until 2 December 1999. This delay arose over the divergent positions of the Ulster Unionists and Sinn Féin over the issue of decommissioning. On the one hand, David Trimble adopted a 'guns for government' stance which sought IRA decommissioning in advance of an Executive being formed including Sinn Féin, while on the other hand, Sinn Féin was adamant that the Agreement did not require decommissioning in advance of executive formation and that the issue would be dealt with in the context of full implementation of the accord.

The gridlock over executive formation continued throughout the remainder of 1998 and most of 1999. On 15 July 1999 the UUP refused to take part in the operation of d'Hondt to allocate ministerial positions and form a government. The stalemate eventually led to a review undertaken by former US Senator George Mitchell which recommended the decommissioning of all paramilitary weapons by 22 May 2000 and would be overseen by the **Independent International Commission on Decommissioning (IICD)**. A number of steps were agreed towards the end of 1999 with the IRA pledging to appoint a representative to the IICD and Trimble lodging a post-dated resignation letter to have effect in the absence of decommissioning by February 2000. Following an agreed choreography between the parties executive formation took place under the d'Hondt procedure on 29 November 1999.

How successful was the Executive?

It is important to consider that the new Northern Ireland Executive included four parties that held divergent views over Northern Ireland's constitutional status and the objectives of the Agreement. Certainly, there appears to have been some commitment on the part of the UUP and SDLP as the main negotiators of the 1998 Agreement to promote reconciliation and accommodation as the basis of the new political dispensation. Significantly, however, in addition to these two more 'moderate' parties the coalition included republicans in government for the first time and the DUP remained opposed to the system. So how successful was the Executive? What were the particular challenges it faced?

The Executive faced a number of particular challenges during its operation from 2 December 1999 to 14 October 2002. One issue was that the parties were not overly prepared for government and lacked a policy strategy that could be implemented by the new Executive. The Agreement stated that the Assembly would have responsibility for the matters under the control of the six direct rule departments and that the Executive would consist of the First Minister and Deputy First Minister and 'up to ten Ministers with Departmental responsibilities'. Thus, it was then up to the parties to agree the final number and functions of the various portfolios. The period from June 1998 until February 1999 was taken up with inter-party discussions on departmental remits without much focus on what the ministers would do when in office. The first Programme for Government was eventually agreed on 6 March 2001, which outlined the Executive's policy commitments.

The 'half in, half out' position of the DUP

A particular issue for the practice of power sharing was the 'semidetached' position of the DUP. Although the anti-Agreement party had decided to take its Assembly seats and ministerial seats on the Executive, it remained one step removed from the operation of the coalition as a collective entity. Thus, its two ministers boycotted the meetings of the Executive 'cabinet'. The DUP also adopted a singular position for a governing party in that it opposed decisions which were supposed to have been agreed by the Executive. This included voting against successive Programmes for Government and budgets on the floor of the Assembly. The DUP's 'half in, half out' approach was further bolstered by the rotation of its ministerial portfolios among party members (see table 7.1, above). Interestingly, the other Executive parties displayed a readiness and flexibility to accommodate the DUP position. Certainly, the Office of First Minister and Deputy First Minister (OFMDFM) was keen to stress that the DUP's non-attendance at Executive meetings would not adversely affect the Executive's work or the delivery of public services.

Ministerial autonomy

An important critique of the Executive during the first mandate of the Assembly following the 1998 Agreement is that ministers had considerable autonomy and had the capacity to take decisions against the wishes of their coalition colleagues and the Assembly. This relates to the convention of **ministerial accountability** whereby ministers are accountable to parliament for the decisions of his/her department. As outlined in Chapter 8, the Northern Ireland (St Andrews Agreement) Act 2006 made a number of amendments to the institutional rules of power sharing which aimed to constrain the capacity of ministers to go on 'solo runs'.

Two particular episodes are often cited to demonstrate the degree of ministerial autonomy during the period 1999 to 2002: (1) the decision of Health Minister Bairbre de Brún (Sinn Féin) on the issue of maternity services; and (2) the announcement by Education Minister Martin McGuinness (Sinn Féin) on the abolition of the '11-plus' post-primary transfer test. In relation to de Brún's decision, the minister opted to locate the Belfast maternity services at Royal Victoria Hospital in west Belfast (a predominately nationalist area) rather than at the City Hospital in the south of the city. Her decision was opposed by the Health Committee and a vote in the Assembly. The minister's decision was eventually ruled unlawful at a judicial review in December 2000 on the grounds that she had failed to consult properly with the Assembly.

The announcement by the Education Minister Martin McGuinness of the abolition of the '11-plus' post-primary transfer exam is also cited as an example of ministers acting with considerable autonomy. McGuinness launched a consultation on the future of post-primary review, but sided with the Burns Report recommendation for the abolition of academic selection despite a majority in his department's household survey supporting the retention of academic selection and grammar schools. The issue became even more controversial when McGuinness made the announcement to abolish the '11-plus' just days before the suspension of the institutions in October 2002. These two examples are often cited as evidence of the lack of ministerial accountability and a critique of power sharing under the 1998 Agreement.

Inter-party tensions
There were also difficult inter-party and inter-personal relations within the Executive. For instance, it is widely known that the First Minister David Trimble and Deputy First Minister Seamus Mallon had a somewhat tense working relationship. Relations between the top two ministers were somewhat better between Trimble and Mark Durkan who replaced Mallon as Deputy First Minister in November 2001. Significantly, the lack of more positive relations within the OFMDFM belies the 'jointery' that was intended at the centre of the administration.

The governing parties also took each other to court in a series of legal challenges and judicial reviews, again symptomatic of the difficult inter-party relations. For instance, Trimble took the step of banning Sinn Féin ministers from attending the North–South Ministerial Council as a sanction measure over the failure of the IRA to engage with the IICD, against which Sinn Féin launched a legal challenge. On 30 January 2001 a high court judge ruled that the ban was unlawful but stipulated that Trimble could nominate SDLP ministers, not necessarily Sinn Féin ministers, to the meetings to comply with the cross-community requirement.

The strains between the OFMDFM and the DUP also gave rise to action in the courts. In June 2000, Trimble and Mallon announced they would not issue executive papers to the DUP ministers as a matter of course in order to maintain cabinet confidentiality. The issue later came to a head when papers in relation to the policy of free public transport for the elderly were withheld from the DUP ministers in February 2001. In the high court a judge upheld the right of the OFMDFM to withhold information but the decision was overturned on appeal in January 2002 when the judge held that DUP ministers Gregory Campbell and Maurice Morrow had a legitimate expectation to receive the same papers as other ministers.

In assessing the record of the power-sharing coalition that existed for less than three years, it is important to accredit some measure of success to the administration. Although the parties were not used to governing – a symptom of the region's history of direct rule from Westminster – they did agree on a number of important policy developments during this period. These include the policy of free public transport for the elderly, investment in students, the decision to appoint a children's commissioner, the publication of a new regional strategy and the launch of the Review of Public Administration. The Executive also displayed competent and prompt handling of the foot and mouth crisis led by the Agriculture Minister Bríd Rodgers, which included a 'joined-up' approach with other departments and with London and Dublin. The Executive was, however, hampered by a lack of trust and lacked strategic direction in some important policy areas, particularly in relation to a community relations strategy.

The Civic Forum

Under Strand One, the 1998 Agreement also established the Civic Forum, a consultative body comprising of representatives of the business, trades union and voluntary sectors in Northern Ireland. The objective of this new institution was for the representatives to meet and discuss social, economic and cultural issues. The establishment of the Civic Forum was delayed, however, and it met for the first time with sixty members in October 2000. The Civic Forum is a notable institution in the sense that it gives people from outside political parties the opportunity to influence the work of the Assembly. The Civic Forum did not meet following suspension of the institutions in October 2002.

Strand Two: north–south cooperation

An important feature of the institutional architecture of the 1998 Agreement is that the new structures were not based on just internal power sharing, but also on institutions to reflect both north–south and east–west relations. As O'Leary argues, the Agreement is more than consociational due to its external dimensions: 'It is one made with national and not just ethnic or religious communities, and it is one endorsed by both leaders and the led . . . the Agreement establishes an internal consociation built within overarching confederal and federal institutions'.[5] Strand Two refers to the north–south institutions in the form of the North–South Ministerial Council and the north–south bodies; Strand Three provides for east–west relations between the UK and the Republic of Ireland.

The negotiations in April 1998 on Strand Two institutions were fairly protracted. On the one hand, the SDLP was adamant that the 'Irish dimension' was a crucial part of any deal. Thus, the SDLP wanted to see an institution established with executive powers rather than a 'talking shop'. On the other hand, however, the possibility of a strong north–south institution was highly contentious for the UUP, who did not want to see ministers from the Irish Republic having a say in the internal affairs of Northern Ireland.

The North–South Ministerial Council and north–south bodies

Under the 1998 Agreement the North–South Ministerial Council (NSMC) is comprised of ministers from both the Northern Ireland Executive and the Irish Government. The NSMC is charged with the objective of developing consultation, cooperation and action on the island of Ireland. Thus, ministers would cooperate on areas of mutual benefit to both regions and the north–south bodies would implement policy decisions. It is important to note the significance of the NSMC: the institution was a crucial symbol for nationalists of the now institutionalised 'Irish dimension'. In contrast, unionists were fearful that the NSMC would create a powerful role for itself; they wanted its work to be consultative and not executive and that the Assembly would have control over the direction of its ministers in the NSMC. After much discussion a compromise was reached between the UUP and the SDLP: the Ulster Unionists succeeded in limiting the power of the NSMC in return for full executive power sharing, an important goal for the SDLP.[6]

The Good Friday Agreement also provided for six north–south bodies operating on an all-island basis which were accountable to the NSMC, Dáil Éireann and the Northern Ireland Assembly. The bodies formally established by the two governments in March 1999 were: Waterways Ireland; the Food Safety Promotion Board; InterTrade Ireland; Special European Union Programmes Body; The Language Body (consisting of *Foras na Gaeilge* and *Tha Boord o Ulster-Scotch*); and the Foyle, Carlingford and Irish Lights Commission. In addition to the six cross-border implementation bodies the two governments and polit-ical parties agreed on six 'Areas for Cooperation'. These Areas were agreed at the inaugural meeting of the NSMC in December 1999 as: Agriculture; Education; Environment; Health; Tourism; and Transport and were to be developed via existing bodies.

Assessment of Strand Two
The operation of Strand Two was, at times, contentious. As mentioned above, First Minister David Trimble refused to nominate Sinn Féin ministers to the NSMC due to the difficulties over IRA decommissioning. Moreover, the two DUP ministers boycotted the work of the NSMC. In practice, however, it appears that the north–south institutions were not as significant as unionists had feared or nationalists had hoped. The NSMC's activities focused on sectoral and plenary meetings. While the plenary meetings reviewed the general direction of north–south cooperation and the work of the NSMC, sectoral meetings were concerned with the work of the six imple-

mentation bodies. In terms of the activity of the six implementation bodies, InterTrade Ireland was one of the most proactive bodies in its efforts to encourage trade development across the island. Compared with the work of the implementation bodies progress was slower with regard to the six areas designated for cooperation. The most notable examples of cooperation took place in the areas of tourism, with Tourism Ireland established in December 2000, and agriculture, particularly in relation to the handling of the foot and mouth crisis.

An interesting point concerns the status of the NSMC and the north–south bodies in the aftermath of the suspension of the institutions in October 2002. Significantly, the Agreement states that the Assembly and the NSMC are 'mutually inter-dependent, and that one cannot successfully function without the other'. Indeed, this interdependence of the institutions demonstrates the novelty of the Agreement's institutional architecture. It is significant that in the postsuspension period the two governments decided to sustain the north–south institutions. The NSMC and the north–south bodies operated on a 'care and maintenance' basis undertaken by the British and Irish Governments. The two governments were determined to focus on restoring the institutions under the Agreement while also continuing with the work already undertaken and planned for north–south cooperation. Thus, north–south cooperation continued in the suspension period; a problematic issue for unionists who remained suspicious that the British and Irish Governments would further develop north–south cooperation in the absence of control from the Assembly.

Strand Three: east–west relations

Strand Three represents another aspect of the Good Friday Agreement's innovative institutional structure which established two new institutions to reflect east–west relations: the British–Irish Council (BIC) and the British–Irish Inter-Governmental Conference (BIIC). The inclusion of east–west institutions sets the 1998 Agreement apart from previous political initiatives as this was the first time relations between the different parts of the UK and Ireland were given institutional effect. It is important to consider that the east–west institutions had a particular rationale for unionists. As Graham Walker points out, the BIC was designed as a 'balance' to the north–south provisions of

Strand Two: 'Whereas Strand Two was shaped towards Irish nationalist demands and aspirations, so Strand Three, especially the BIC, was conceived to offer reassurance to Ulster unionists'.[7] Walker notes that the inclusion of the BIC in the Agreement appears to have been 'fundamental to the Ulster Unionist Party's acceptance of the whole package'.

The British–Irish Council

Under the Agreement the BIC aims to 'promote the harmonious and mutually beneficial development of the totality of relationships among the peoples of these islands'. Established on 2 December 1999, the BIC is made up of representatives from the British and Irish Governments and devolved administrations in Scotland, Wales and Northern Ireland, and the Isle of Man, Jersey and Guernsey. The members consult and exchange information on areas of mutual benefit. At the time of writing the BIC had eight agreed work sectors: Misuse of Drugs; Environment; Social Inclusion; Transport; Knowledge Economy; Tourism; Telemedicine; and Minority and Lesser-Used Languages. At regular meetings the members exchange views and can embark on measures of practical cooperation in these areas.

Clearly, the BIC has the potential to create new intergovernmental relationships between the different regions. As Walker notes, 'a clause in the Agreement providing for two or more members to develop bilateral or multilateral arrangements between them goes beyond "consultation" into the possibility of "joint decision-making" on matters of mutual interest'.[8] Again, suspension of the institutions did not impact on the meetings of the BIC where the topics under discussion and relating to Northern Ireland were represented by the British Government.

The British–Irish Intergovernmental Conference

The BIIC was also established in December 1999. Its rationale was to institutionalise bilateral cooperation between the UK and Ireland, and it replaced the Anglo-Irish Conference which was set up by the Anglo-Irish Agreement of 1985. Importantly, the institution reflected the continuing involvement of the Republic of Ireland in the internal affairs of Northern Ireland. Cooperation between the two governments would focus on matters of mutual interest relating to a fairly extensive range of non-devolved issues including policing, criminal justice and the prison service.

In the run-up to the restoration of devolution in May 2007 the two governments used the BIIC as a vehicle to review political developments and the security situation in Northern Ireland. They also discussed issues relating to policing and justice, human rights and equality and north–south and east–west relations.

The decommissioning stalemate

The decommissioning of paramilitary weapons has been one of the most problematic issues affecting Northern Ireland politics since the ceasefires of 1994 and 1997 and the signing of the Agreement in 1998. Certainly, a lack of progress on decommissioning has been detrimental to the implementation of the Agreement. As Tonge notes, decommissioning, 'long seen as inevitable in informed republican circles, was sufficiently protracted to place the devolved institutions in jeopardy'.[9]

As noted above, decommissioning was a significant issue in the run-up to executive formation which eventually took place on 29 November 1999. UUP leader David Trimble wanted IRA decommissioning to take place prior to executive formation including Sinn Féin; republicans, however, stressed that decommissioning should take place as part of the full implementation of the Agreement. The Agreement had a section on Decommissioning which stated that parties must:

> continue to work constructively and in good faith with the Independent Commission, and to use any influence they may have, to achieve the decommissioning of all paramilitary arms within two years following endorsement in referendums North and South of the agreement and in the context of the implementation of the overall settlement.[10]

A compromise between the UUP and Sinn Féin positions was reached following a Review led by former US Senator George Mitchell from September to November 1999. The Mitchell Review suggested that decommissioning of all paramilitary weapons should take place by 22 May 2000 and in a manner determined by the IICD. In the wake of the Review the IRA pledged to appoint a representative to the IICD.

Trimble then agreed to go into government with Sinn Féin and lodged a post-dated resignation letter to take effect should no decommissioning occur by February 2000. The lack of movement by the IRA by that date, however, led the Secretary of State Peter Mandelson to suspend the institutions.

On 6 May 2000 the IRA issued a statement on its commitment to 'a just and lasting peace' followed by resumption of contact with the IICD. The IRA announced it would 'initiate a process that will completely and verifiably put IRA arms beyond use' and that the two independent international inspectors, the former Finnish President Martti Ahtisaari and former ANC secretary-general Cyril Ramaphosa, would be allowed to examine arms dumps on 26 June 2000.[11] Trimble then won majority support from the Ulster Unionist Council to re-enter the Executive with Sinn Féin and devolution was restored on 29 May 2000.

Trimble resigned as First Minister on 1 July 2001 due to the slow rate of progress, and Secretary of State John Reid moved to suspend the institutions on 10 August in an attempt to resolve the impasse. Following another technical suspension on 21 September and continued failure over IRA weapons, the three UUP ministers resigned from the Executive on 18 October. On 23 October the IRA announced the beginning of the decommissioning process saying the move was in order 'to save the peace process' and 'persuade others of our genuine intentions'.[12] The UUP ministerial positions were then reinstalled and the re-election of Trimble as First Minister with Mark Durkan as Deputy First Minister took place on 6 November 2001. The second act of decommissioning took place on 8 April 2002 which the IICD described as 'substantial'.[13]

The Executive faced mounting difficulties throughout its period in office. The already fraught unionist–republican relations over decommissioning increased in the wake of the 'Colombia Three' episode in August 2001 and the removal of Special Branch files from Castlereagh police barracks in March 2002. There were also considerable divisions within unionism which threatened Trimble's already delicate position as UUP leader. By October 2002 the unveiling of an alleged republican spy-ring at Stormont took over with police raids on homes of republicans and Sinn Féin party offices at Stormont on 4 October. On 8 October the DUP issued a statement that the party's two ministers were set to resign and Trimble issued an ultimatum to Blair that unless Sinn Féin was expelled from the Executive the UUP ministers would also resign. The institutions were duly suspended on 14 October 2002 for the fourth time in less than three years.

The process of IRA decommissioning has been one of 'stops and starts'. Clearly, the slow progress and controversy over decommissioning highlights the fact that republicans and unionists had very different views and expectations on the pace of change. In the aftermath of suspension decommissioning continued to dominate politics in Northern Ireland. The third act of IRA decommissioning took place on 21 October 2003 amid some controversy, as the UUP was disappointed over the lack of transparency in relation to the exact configuration of arsenal destroyed.

On 28 July 2005 the IRA issued a statement calling on all IRA units to end the armed campaign and dump their arms. On 26 September 2005 the IICD announced that the IRA had completed the decommissioning of all of their weapons. The focus then shifted to the decommissioning of loyalist weapons; some decommissioning by the LVF took place as a token gesture in 1998 but no further decommissioning was carried out by any of the loyalist paramilitary groups. In the aftermath of full IRA decommissioning, there was no sign that loyalists would follow suit. In March 2007 the British Government announced that it would provide £1.2 million for a project to encourage the UDA to move away from violence and criminal activity. Thus, it was hoped that a transformation of loyalists groups would result in the decommissioning of their weapons.

Police reform

Policing is often a highly contentious issue in a deeply divided society. Divisions over policing have been evident in Northern Ireland as nationalists and republicans viewed the RUC as illegitimate while unionists supported the police force. The Agreement acknowledged the different perceptions of the police on the part of the two communities and stated that 'the agreement provides the opportunity for a new beginning to policing in Northern Ireland with a police service capable of attracting and sustaining support from the community as a whole'.[14] Under the Agreement an independent commission was

Box 7.1 Decommissioning timeline

September–November 1999 Mitchell Review
11 February 2000 Peter Mandelson suspended the devolved institutions
6 May 2000 IRA announced that it would commence a process to put weapons beyond use
29 May 2000 Devolution restored
1 July 2001 David Trimble resigned as First Minister
10 August 2001 John Reid suspended institutions for 24 hours
21 September 2001 John Reid suspended institutions for 24 hours
23 October 2001 IRA announced beginning of decommissioning
8 April 2002 Second act of IRA decommissioning
14 October 2002 Fourth and final suspension
21 October 2003 Third act of IRA decommissioning
28 July 2005 IRA statement for all IRA units to stand down and hand over weapons
26 September 2005 IICD statement that IRA decommissioning had been completed
22 March 2007 British Government announced funding for the UDA to move away from violence and crime

established to make recommendations for future policing in Northern Ireland. This commission became the Independent Commission on Policing for Northern Ireland led by former governor of Hong Kong and Chairman of the Conservative Party, Chris Patten.

The Patten Commission published its Report, 'A New Beginning: Policing in Northern Ireland' in September 1999. The Report included an extensive list of proposals for reform of the RUC. Recommendations included improving the accountability of the police by creating a Policing Board whose primary statutory function would be to hold the Chief Constable and the police service publicly to account. The Commission also advocated greater dialogue between the police and the local community through the creation of District Policing Partnership Boards in each district council area.

A significant recommendation was for the creation of a Police Ombudsman post to investigate complaints against the police. The Report stated that the Office of the Police Ombudsman should be 'an important institution in the governance of Northern Ireland . . .

The Ombudsman should take initiatives, not merely react to specific complaints received. He/she should exercise the power to initiate inquiries or investigations even if no specific complaint has been received'.[15] It should be noted that the Office of the Police Ombudsman has been very proactive in its investigations, at times focusing on extremely contentious issues as demonstrated by the 'Operation Ballast Report' published in 2007 which explored allegations of police collusion with loyalist paramilitaries in north Belfast.

The Patten Report also recommended that the Full-Time Reserve would be phased out, while creating an enlarged Part-Time Reserve. In relation to the future size of the force, the Report suggested that over the following ten years the total number of full time officers should be reduced to 7,500. A highly controversial proposal related to the recruitment of police officers. To address the disproportionate number of Catholic officers (8 per cent in 1998), the Report proposed that a recruitment profile of 50 per cent Protestant and 50 per cent Catholic should be drawn over a ten-year period. The 50:50 quota has proven contentious in recent years but is generally accepted to be a necessary measure to increase the number of nationalists and republicans in the police force. Finally, the Patten Commission recommended a number of changes in relation to the culture, ethos and symbols of the RUC. This included changing the name of the force which was eventually settled as the Police Service of Northern Ireland (PSNI) and came into being in November 2001. The Report also proposed that the reformed police service should have a new badge and symbols not associated with either the British or Irish states. The agreed emblem features a St Patrick's cross surrounded by six symbols: a crown; harp; shamrock; laurel leaf; torch; and scales of justice.

The response of the parties to the general principle of police reform and the particular reforms recommended by the Patten Commission were mixed. On the one hand, unionists had supported the RUC which was a predominantly Protestant and unionist force. Thus, the emotive issues arising from the Agreement in relation to police reform as well as the release of paramilitary prisoners and the slow pace of decommissioning were difficult for the unionist community. In particular, unionists were opposed to the name change of the RUC and removal of British symbols. On the other hand, nationalists and republicans had viewed the RUC as discriminatory and

Box 7.2 Main reforms to policing in Northern Ireland

Creation of a Policing Board
Creation of District Policing Partnerships
Creation of the Police Ombudsman for Northern Ireland
Full-Time Reserve to be phased out
Part-Time Reserve to be enlarged
Total number of full time officers to be reduced to 7,500
50:50 recruitment quota for equal number of Protestant and Catholic recruits
Name change from Royal Ulster Constabulary to Police Service of Northern Ireland
New badge and flag

illegitimate. They pointed to the issue of collusion between the RUC and loyalist paramilitaries, later highlighted by the Stevens Inquiry in April 2003.

It is important to note, however, that the SDLP and Sinn Féin held divergent views on the pace and extent of reforms required. While the SDLP advocated sweeping reforms of the RUC, Sinn Féin wanted it to disband, rather than simply reform the old police force. The SDLP welcomed the Patten recommendations and looked forward to their full implementation. In 2001 the party joined the Policing Board and gave its support to the PSNI. Sinn Féin's reaction was less welcoming than that of the SDLP. The party did, however, signal that full implementation of the Patten recommendations would be a potential basis for a new beginning. As we will see in the next chapter, the Sinn Féin *ard fheis* in January 2007 voted to support the PSNI which signalled another departure for policing in Northern Ireland.

••

✔ What you should have learnt from reading this chapter

• The Good Friday/Belfast Agreement established a novel institutional architecture based on internal power sharing and new north–south and east–west political arrangements.

• The Northern Ireland Assembly was fairly successful and the work of the statutory committees was notable in relation to their scrutinising role.

- The Northern Ireland Executive encountered a number of difficulties in relation to the lack of inter-party trust and the 'half in, half out' position of the DUP.

- The issue of IRA decommissioning was a particular plague on the administration as lack of progress constantly threatened the operation of the devolved administration

- The reform of policing was also contentious; the Patten recommendations were crucial for nationalists and republicans and a difficult, emotive issue for unionists

Glossary of key terms

Cross-community voting Procedures used in the Assembly whereby decisions require the approval of both unionists and nationalists; the Agreement specifies two alternative procedures: 'parallel consent' and 'weighted majority' voting (see above, 'Strand One: the Northern Ireland Assembly'.

D'Hondt A proportional method often used for allocating offices to parties according to their strength in the legislature. It is used in Northern Ireland to allocate ministerial seats to the Executive. The party with the largest number of seats gets first pick of the portfolios and then its seat share is divided by two. The party with the next largest number of seats gets the next ministry and so on, using a series of divisors (1,2,3. . .n) until all ministries are allocated.

Independent International Commission on Decommissioning (IICD) Established by the British and Irish Governments on 26 August 1997 with the objective of facilitating the destruction of paramilitary weapons and ammunition. For IICD reports and statements see http://cain.ulst.ac.uk/events/peace/decommission/iicdreports.htm.

Ministerial accountability A convention of parliamentary democracy where government ministers are accountable to parliament for the decisions of his/her department. A twin convention relates to cabinet collective responsibility in which all ministers support government policies.

Single transferable vote (STV) Proportional representation (PR) electoral system used to elect the 108 members of the Northern Ireland Assembly (six MLAs in each of the eighteen constituencies). The voter chooses as many or as few candidates he/she wishes as listed on the constituency ballot paper. The voter ranks the candidate with 1 for first preference, 2 for second choice, 3 for third choice and so on. The ballot is allocated first to the preferred candidate. If this candidate has more votes than required by the quota, his/her surplus is transferred to other candidates as expressed by the voter. The votes of eliminated candidates are also transferred to remaining candidates. The transfer of votes continues until all posts have been filled.

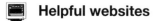 **Likely examination questions**

- Discuss the institutional architecture of the Good Friday/Belfast Agreement.

- What challenges were faced by the Northern Ireland Assembly and Executive in the period 1998–2002?

 Helpful websites

British Irish Council: http://www1.british-irishcouncil.org

Northern Ireland Assembly: http://www.niassembly.gov.uk

Northern Ireland Executive: http://www.northernireland.gov.uk

North–South Ministerial Council:
http://www.northsouthministerialcouncil.org

Conflict Archive on the Internet: http://cain.ulst.ac.uk

BBC Online: IRA statements available at http://news.bbc.co.uk/2/
hi/uk_news/northern_ireland/4607913.stm

Suggestions for further reading

Thomas Hennessey, *The Northern Ireland Peace Process: Ending the Troubles?*, Dublin: Gill and Macmillan, 2000.

Joseph Ruane and Jennifer Todd (eds), *After the Good Friday Agreement: Analysing Political Change in Northern Ireland*, Dublin: University College Dublin Press, 1999.

Jonathan Tonge, *The New Northern Irish Politics?*, Basingstoke: Palgrave Macmillan, 2005.

Rick Wilford (ed.), *Aspects of the Belfast Agreement*, Oxford: Oxford University Press, 2001.

Towards Restored Devolution

Contents

Overview

The chapter explores political developments in Northern Ireland following the suspension of the institutions and return of direct rule in October 2002. It discusses the political stalemate following the 2003 Assembly election and the extent of unionist disaffection with the implementation of the Good Friday/Belfast Agreement. The chapter presents the proposals on the part of the political parties and the British and Irish Governments for restored devolution in relation to the Review of the Agreement in 2004. It then highlights the important amendments to the 1998 Agreement made in the Northern Ireland (St Andrews Agreement) Act 2006. Finally, the chapter charts the political events surrounding the 2007 Assembly election, the agreement between the DUP and Sinn Féin and the restoration of devolved power sharing on 8 May 2007.

Key issues to be covered in this chapter

- The different forms of devolution in the UK
- Stalemate during the post-suspension period
- Efforts made by the British and Irish Governments to restore devolution
- Significance of the St Andrews Agreement which made several changes to the Good Friday/Belfast Agreement
- Events that led to the restoration of devolved power sharing, including the significance of Sinn Féin's support for the police and the DUP's willingness to form a government with republicans
- Early successes of the power-sharing executive formed on 8 May 2007

Devolution in the UK

Devolution was established in the UK by the Labour Government at the end of the 1990s. This process of constitutional reform radically changed the political landscape of the UK. The previous chapter outlined the institutional framework for devolved government in Northern Ireland under the Good Friday/Belfast Agreement. Before exploring the political developments following suspension of the institutions in October 2002, this section presents the similarities and differences between the devolved structures in Northern Ireland, Scotland and Wales.

Northern Ireland

In Northern Ireland, power was transferred to a Northern Ireland Assembly elected by proportional representation (STV) with 108 MLAs. Devolution in Northern Ireland meant a power-sharing administration, formed on 29 November 1999 between the four main parties: the UUP; the SDLP; the DUP; and Sinn Féin. Importantly, devolution in Northern Ireland was not just about the internal arrangements for power sharing, it was also about a peace agreement and addressing the important north–south and east–west relations via the North–South Ministerial Council and the British–Irish Council, respectively.

The Northern Ireland Act 1998 contains three categories of legislative power: excepted; reserved; and transferred. While excepted matters relate to defence, immigration policy, currency and international relations, reserved matters include policing and criminal law. All other matters are transferred matters which deal with the areas of domestic affairs such as health, education and the environment which were handled by the Northern Ireland departments under direct rule.

Scotland

Devolution in Scotland established the Scottish Parliament with 129 Members of the Scottish Parliament elected by the mixed member proportional representation system and the Scottish Executive. Under the mixed member proportional representation system, seventy-three MSPs represent individual geographical constituencies elected by 'first past the post' with an additional fifty-six members returned from eight additional member regions, each electing seven MSPs. The first two

Scottish Parliaments elections – in 1999 and 2003 – led to coalition government between Labour and the Liberal Democrats. The third election, however, in May 2007, resulted in an electoral victory for the Scottish National Party (SNP) with Alex Salmond becoming First Minister. The first time the SNP was in government, Salmond pledged his continued support for the goal of an independent Scotland.

The Scottish Parliament has general competence over all matters not expressly reserved to Westminster. Reserved matters include matters such foreign affairs, defence and national security, but also include company law, competition policy and industrial relations and the welfare state. A notable difference between Scottish devolution and that in Northern Ireland and Wales is that the Scottish Parliament can raise or lower the rate of income tax by up to 3p in the pound.

Wales
In Wales, the arrangements for devolution are weaker than in both Northern Ireland and Scotland. The Government of Wales Act 1998 created the National Assembly with sixty Assembly members elected under the mixed member proportional representation system. Although the Assembly is a legislature, it does not have primary legislative or fiscal powers, as these powers have been reserved by Westminster. The legislative powers of the Assembly are, therefore, fairly limited as it can only make secondary or subordinate legislation in areas within its competence and transferred from ministers, primarily the Secretary of State. Since it was established in 1999 the Assembly has been pressing for additional powers and to have the same devolved powers as Scotland.

Proposals for executive devolution were put forward in the Government of Wales Act 2006 which would allow the Assembly to acquire enhanced legislative powers for matters approved by Parliament, with full legislative powers if approved in a referendum in the future. At the May 2007 Welsh Assembly election, Labour failed to win a majority. After two months of negotiations the Welsh nationalist party Plaid Cymru entered government for the first time in a coalition with Labour. Part of the agreement between the two parties committed the new coalition to work towards a positive referendum vote on full legislative powers within four years.

Table 8.1 Different forms of devolution in the UK

Type of devolution	Scotland: Parliament	Wales: National Assembly	Northern Ireland: Assembly
Administrative devolution – Manage services (e.g. education, health) – Allocate funds	Yes	Yes	Yes
Legislative devolution – Power to make, repeal, amend laws	Yes	No (can make secondary legislation in areas transferred from the Secretary of State)	Yes
Fiscal autonomy – Power to raise taxes or vary taxation independently	Yes	No	No

Suspension and stalemate

As the previous chapter outlined, the Northern Ireland Assembly, which operated from the devolution of power on 2 December 1999, was subject to a number of suspensions, principally over the issue of IRA decommissioning. In October 2002 the institutions were suspended by the British Government for the fourth and final time. The circumstances of this suspension came as a result of an alleged republican spy-ring at Parliament Buildings, Stormont. The crisis led Secretary of State John Reid to trigger suspension and the reintroduction of direct rule from Westminster.

In the aftermath of suspension the British and Irish Governments continued in their efforts to reinstate inter-party negotiations and restore devolution. In April 2003 the two governments published a Joint Declaration which called on the parties to meet their obligations under the Good Friday Agreement. The document stated that for trust to be established among the parties 'it must be clear that the transition from violence to exclusively peaceful and democratic means is being brought to an unambiguous and definitive conclusion'. All parties were called upon to demonstrate their 'commitment to the operation of political institutions that are characterised by durability, effectiveness and inclusiveness'.[1]

In October 2003 a number of steps were taken in an effort to reach agreement between the Ulster Unionists and Sinn Féin. On 21 October the IICD published a statement that verified the IRA's third act of decommissioning. While General John de Chastelain stated that the amount of weapons was larger than the previous amount, the IRA requirement for confidentiality prevented him from providing a list of the weapons and ammunition put beyond use. The absence of specific detail on the decommissioning disappointed the Ulster Unionists and ultimately prevented the realisation of agreement between the two parties and restoration of the institutions. Failure of this attempt to secure agreement led to a lengthy suspension, particularly in the wake of the 2003 Assembly election.

Assembly election November 2003

With the Assembly suspended since October 2002, an election had been planned for May 2003. The election was postponed, however, as it was felt unlikely that a new Assembly would get up and running thereafter. Following a delay of several months, polling day was finally called for 26 November 2003. The 2003 Assembly election is significant as the results changed the potential for restored devolution. The DUP and Sinn Féin firmly cemented their position as the largest parties of their respective blocs.

The DUP made the most gains as the party increased its Assembly seat share from twenty to thirty seats and won just over 25 per cent of the first preference votes. Sinn Féin also made gains by increasing its seat share by six seats from eighteen to twenty-four. Although the UUP lost just one seat, three members (Jeffrey Donaldson, Arlene Foster and

Norah Beare) later left the party to join the DUP. It was an extremely disappointing election for the SDLP as the party's seat share was reduced from twenty-four to eighteen. The Alliance Party managed to hold its six seats despite winning only 3.7 per cent of the vote. The NIWC was severely disappointed by the loss of both of their seats.

The election results meant that the formation of any new power-sharing executive would have to be agreed by the DUP and Sinn Féin as the two largest parties. Under the Good Friday/Belfast Agreement the post of First Minister would likely go to the DUP while Sinn Féin would take the position of Deputy First Minister. As per the text of the Agreement, the formation of a new executive would require nom-inations and a cross-community vote on the joint premiers. As the DUP was not prepared to vote for a republican as Deputy First Minister, the election results meant that it was potentially even more difficult to restore the Assembly.

It is important to ask why the electorate voted for the two 'extreme' parties rather than the more 'moderate' UUP and SDLP who were the dominant parties in 1998. Were the election results something to do with the Agreement itself? Did the results signify that the elec-torate had become increasingly polarised in the period since the signing of the Agreement? Indeed, was this apparent increased polar-isation the makings of the Agreement? One reading of the election results would suggest that Northern Ireland had become increasingly divided as the electorate opted to support two highly antagonistic parties. There is an argument, however, that the electoral competition between the two communities and the electoral outcomes were more to do with the party system that had existed for many years and not as a result of the implementation of the 1998 Agreement. As Tonge writes, 'Ethnic-bloc party competition owed more to preexist-ing intra-bloc electoral rivalries than the particular nature of the devolved settlement in Northern Ireland'.[2]

Unionist disaffection with the Agreement

It is arguable that an important reason for the 2003 election results, in particular the DUP gains, lie with unionist disaffection with polit-ics and the workings of the 1998 Agreement. Indeed, it appears that there was a growing perception on the part of the unionist commu-nity that the 'peace process' had been about granting concessions to nationalists/republicans. Tonge notes that 'The failure of the GFA to persuade a sufficiently large majority of unionists of its merits led to the demise of the Assembly'.[3] As noted in Chapter 6, an exit poll of the 1998 referendum on the Agreement recorded that 55 per cent of unionists voted in favour of the Agreement. It is also arguable that the ongoing debacle over decommissioning, paramilitary and criminal activity on the part of the IRA and the alleged republican spy-ring contributed to the sense of unionist disaffection.

The view of unionist disenchantment with political developments is borne out by the Northern Ireland Life and Times survey on political attitudes.[4] For instance, an interesting survey question asked respondents whether they believed nationalists or unionists had benefited more from the Good Friday Agreement. In 2003, 70 per cent of Protestant respondents believed that nationalists benefited more than unionists. Conversely, 0 per cent of Protestants believed that unionists benefited more than nationalists. In response to the question how would you vote if the Good Friday Agreement referendum was held again, only 28 per cent of Protestants said they would vote 'yes' compared with 74 per cent of Catholic respondents.

Review of the Agreement

In the absence of inter-party agreement, the parties were called to Stormont at the beginning of 2004 to undertake a Review of the institutional arrangements as provided for in the Agreement. Indeed, the 1998 Agreement stipulated that 'the two governments and the parties in the Assembly will convene a conference four years after the Agreement comes into effect, to review and report on its operation'.[5]

Several political parties put forward detailed proposals for reform of the institutions under the Agreement. The Alliance Party's submission, 'Agenda for Democracy', was notable in that its recommendations departed considerably from the provisions of the 1998 Agreement. For instance, Alliance claimed that the Agreement had institutionalised sectarianism in Northern Ireland. In particular, the party was critical of the communal designation system for MLAs whereby members were obliged to designate as 'unionist', 'nationalist' or 'other'. Alliance also proposed that government formation should take place as a result of inter-party negotiation rather than under the d'Hondt procedure (see glossary in Chapter 7). The party's rationale was that a more 'voluntary' type of arrangement would promote more cooperation between the parties; they would have to negotiate with one another and would not simply be guaranteed ministerial seats based on their strength in the Assembly.

The DUP's submission to the Review, 'Devolution Now', was also interesting in that the party also very clearly preferred a power-sharing government formed by whatever parties could agree and guarantee a key vote majority in the Assembly. In agreement with Alliance, executive formation would not happen by way of d'Hondt. The DUP stressed that for any future executive including republicans to take office, the IRA would have to complete decommissioning and end all paramilitary and criminal activity. The party also wanted ministers to be more accountable to the Assembly and not have the capacity to do 'solo runs' as claimed in relation to the previous administration 1999–2002.

The other parties' submissions were arguably not as significant in terms of proposed changes to the workings of the institutions. Sinn Féin called for the full implementation of the Agreement, the stability of the institutions, equality and human rights and the expansion of north–south cooperation. The Ulster Unionist Party did not advance proposals to the Review in relation to institutional reform; for David Trimble, decommissioning was the principal issue to be resolved and there was no justification for talking about institutional reform in the absence of complete decommissioning by the IRA. Unsurprisingly, given its commitment to the Agreement, the SDLP was opposed to what might be perceived as 'renegotiation' and remained committed to fully inclusive power sharing.

Following the Review of the Agreement the British and Irish Governments produced their own proposals, the 'Comprehensive Agreement', in December 2004. The two governments had attempted to secure agreement between the DUP and Sinn Féin and the document included potential statements from those two parties in the event of an agreement. The negotiations broke down, however, over the issue of IRA decommissioning. While the DUP wanted photographs of decommissioning and full transparency of the weapons and ammunition destroyed, such requirements were unacceptable to the IRA. Interestingly, the Comprehensive Agreement proposals included a number of amendments to the 1998 Agreement in respect of ministerial accountability. It was a particular objective of the DUP for any new administration to operate via new rules so that ministers would not have the capacity to pursue policies without the support of the wider Executive as arguably took place under the previous administration. As we will see later in this chapter, the issue of ministerial accountability was revisited in the St Andrews Agreement with a number of significant reforms.

General election May 2005

The failure to secure a deal between the DUP and Sinn Féin in December 2004 led to a period of political stalemate. The mistrust between the two parties was reinforced by events in early 2005, namely allegations of IRA involvement in the Northern Bank robbery and the murder of Belfast man Robert McCartney. All the parties then moved into an election campaign with the UK general election set for May 2005. The parties' election manifestos set out their respective positions in relation to the potential for power sharing. For instance, the DUP manifesto stated that power sharing with Sinn Féin under the d'Hondt procedure or any similar mechanism was out of the question. The party campaigned against fully inclusive power sharing with republicans. Thus, the DUP needed agreement from the SDLP to form a coalition. The SDLP, however, was not prepared to enter a power-sharing government without Sinn Féin.

The results of the 2005 Westminster election were significant as the DUP increased the party's number of MPs from five to nine, while the UUP's seat share fell from six to one (Lady Sylvia Hermon, North Down). It was, therefore, an excellent election for the DUP who now held half of the eighteen Westminster seats and just over a third of the vote. The loss of David Trimble's seat was a particular loss for the UUP. Sinn Féin increased its seat share by one, while the SDLP managed to hold on to its three seats (it kept South Down and Foyle, lost Newry and Armagh but gained South Belfast).

In the aftermath of the general election, efforts continued to resolve the decommissioning issue. In July 2005 the IRA announced an end to their campaign of violence and ordered all units to dump their weapons. Following the fourth act of IRA decommissioning on 26 September the IICD announced that complete IRA decommissioning

Table 8.2 2001 and 2005 Westminster elections

Party	2001 seats	Votes	Share	2005 seats	Votes	Share
DUP	5	181,999	22.5%	9	241,856	33.7%
Sinn Féin	4	175,392	21.7%	5	174,530	24.3%
UUP	6	216,839	26.8%	1	127,314	17.7%
SDLP	3	169,865	21.0%	3	125,626	17.5%

had taken place. The IICD stated, 'we believe that the arms decommissioned represent the totality of the IRA's arsenal'.[6] A Protestant clergyman (the Reverend Harold Good) and a Catholic priest (Father Alec Reid) also witnessed the final act of IRA decommissioning.

St Andrews Agreement 2006

Political stalemate continued throughout 2005 and into 2006. The political climate was reinvigorated, however, with the onset of a fresh round of inter-party talks. An incentive for the parties to agree on devolved power sharing was provided with the British and Irish Governments' threat to use their 'Plan B'. They claimed that if the parties were unable to agree on devolved power sharing, they would draw up alternative arrangements involving greater cooperation between London and Dublin. To provide a more 'neutral' environment, inter-party talks were convened at a hotel in St Andrews, Scotland in October 2006. The discussions failed, however, to secure an agreement among the parties. While all the main parties were in attendance, the focus was on securing agreement between the DUP and Sinn Féin. Despite the lack of agreement among the parties, the British and Irish Governments published their own document, the St Andrews Agreement, with a requirement that the parties should come back in November with an indication as to whether or not they were prepared to proceed on the basis of its provisions.[7]

The St Andrews Agreement set out a timetable for the restoration of devolved power sharing by 26 March 2007. It focused on what Secretary of State for Northern Ireland Peter Hain referred to as the 'twin pillars' of policing and power sharing. In the document the two governments stated that 'support for policing and the rule of law should be extended to every part of the community'. Support for law and order would include 'endorsing fully the Police Service of Northern Ireland and the criminal justice system, actively encouraging everyone of the community to co-operate fully with the PSNI in tackling crime in all areas and actively supporting all the policing and criminal justice institutions, including the Policing Board'.[8] Thus, it was made very clear that political progress would require a commitment from republicans to policing and the rule of law.

It is also of note that the St Andrews Agreement made a number of significant amendments to the 1998 Agreement in relation to the operation of the Strand One institutions, particularly with regard to the issue of ministerial accountability. For instance, an amendment to the Northern Ireland Act 1998 was to be made to introduce a statutory Ministerial Code. Where a decision is not achieved by consensus and a vote is required, any three ministers could trigger a cross-community vote. An amendment to the 1998 Act would provide for thirty MLAs to refer a ministerial decision back to the Executive to consider it within seven days. The main provisions of the St Andrews Agreement, made in the Northern Ireland (St Andrews Agreement) Act 2006 are set out in the table below.

The parties were given until 10 November 2006 to respond to the British and Irish Governments' St Andrews Agreement. By that date the DUP's reaction was neither acceptance nor opposition. Sinn Féin's initial response in early November was qualified support without yet calling a special *ard fheis* on policing. By late November 2006 there was still some discussion over the DUP's preparedness to share power with republicans. Ian Paisley stressed that his party would not enter a power-sharing executive until the conditions were right. As time progressed, it was clear that the DUP and Sinn Féin were prepared to proceed subject to a number of conditions. The DUP wanted a commitment and 'delivery' from Sinn Féin in relation to the party's support for policing and the rule of law. Sinn Féin wanted a clear commitment from the DUP that

Table 8.3 Main provisions of the St Andrews Agreement 2006

Statutory Ministerial Code	Places a duty upon Ministers (not withstanding their executive authority) to act in accordance with the provisions on ministerial accountability of the Code Where a decision of the Executive could not be achieved by consensus and a vote is required, any three Ministers could require it to be taken on a cross-community basis
Assembly referrals for Executive review	Thirty MLAs could refer a ministerial decision back to the Executive within seven days of a ministerial decision Presiding Officer to certify that it concerns an issue of public importance Executive to consider the issue within seven days; second referral could not be made by the Assembly on the same issue
Amendments to the Pledge of Office	Ministers required to participate fully in the Executive and NSMC/BIC and observe the joint nature of the Office of First Minister and Deputy First Minister
Appointment of Ministers in the Executive	Nominations of First Minister and Deputy First Minister without a cross-community vote
Community designation	Assembly members would not be able to change designation for the whole of an Assembly term other than if changing political party
Executive role in preparation for NSMC and BIC meetings	Draft NSMC and BIC papers to be circulated to all Ministers in advance of a NSMC or BIC meeting
Transfer of policing and justice powers	Assembly to report to Secretary of State by 27 March 2008 on preparations for the devolution of policing and justice

the party was committed to forming an inclusive power sharing-government.

In an effort to encourage progress on the part of the DUP and Sinn Féin, Secretary of State for Northern Ireland Peter Hain continued to argue that it was a matter of 'devolution or dissolution'. According to the Northern Ireland Office, the alternative to restored devolution would mean that the Assembly would be dissolved, MLA salaries would stop, and the two governments would progress north–south cooperation under their 'Plan B' with an enhanced role for the Dublin government.

Importantly, the Northern Ireland (St Andrews Agreement) Act 2006 provided for a Transitional Assembly which operated from 22 November 2006 until the restoration of the devolved institutions in May 2007. The Transitional Assembly debated a range of issues including water charges, rate reform, road safety and affordable housing. As the Transitional Assembly was to prepare for the restoration of devolution, a Programme for Government Committee was established to agree priorities for a new Executive. A number of sub-groups of the Committee discussed topics such as economic issues, schools admission, policing and justice and the Review of Public Administration.

Northern Ireland Assembly election March 2007

Following indications from the parties that they were prepared to proceed on the basis of the St Andrews provisions, the two governments announced their decision to hold an Assembly election rather than a referendum on the St Andrews Agreement. With the election set for March 2007, Sinn Féin was required to demonstrate its commitment to the process by supporting the policing structures. After some delay Sinn Féin held its special *ard fheis* on policing in January 2007 where the party's successful motion to change its policy on policing and declare support for the PSNI and the criminal justice system received support from more than 90 per cent of delegates. Following this historic change of direction by republicans the British and Irish Governments hoped that Sinn Féin's move would secure a return to devolution by the deadline of 26 March 2007.

An interesting aspect of the 2007 Northern Ireland Assembly election campaign was the increased focus on more normal 'bread and butter' issues rather than the unionist/nationalist positions regarding Northern Ireland's constitutional status. Throughout the campaign the parties focused on policy issues such as water rates, corporation tax, health, education and the housing market. Interestingly, this focus on social and economic policy led the media to describe the election campaign as somewhat 'lacklustre'. It could be argued, however, that this focus on policy issues illustrated Northern Ireland's incremental move out of conflict towards stable democracy. In contrast to the circumstances of 1998 and 2003, none of the main parties was opposed to the overall direction of the political process. Electoral competition was somewhat different as all of the main parties broadly supported the process as set out in the St Andrews Agreement.

In the run up to the election the DUP stressed that power sharing would not be possible without Sinn Féin 'delivery', which meant support for the PSNI, the criminal justice system and a complete end to paramilitary and criminal activity. For the DUP then, it was up to republicans whether devolution would be restored. The party's policy was a step too far for some party members who were opposed to sharing power with republicans, evidenced by the resignation of Jim Allister MEP and party councillors from Ballymena and Banbridge. Sinn Féin remained committed to power sharing and pledged to expand all-Ireland cooperation. The electoral competition between the DUP and Sinn Féin focused on their respective potential share of ministerial seats in a new Executive; Ian Paisley warned the electorate that votes for parties other than the DUP would risk allowing Martin McGuinness to become First Minister.

The 2007 Assembly election is also interesting in that a number of 'dissidents' contested the election in opposition to the positions of the DUP and Sinn Féin, respectively. The UKUP's Robert McCartney put his name forward in six constituencies and pledged he would represent more than one constituency if elected. McCartney claimed he was offering voters an 'anti-agreement choice' and the potential to prevent the formation of an Executive including Sinn Féin. There were also 'dissidents' in opposition to Sinn Féin's policy on policing evidenced by a number of independents and Republican Sinn Féin candidates on an abstentionist platform. As outlined below, the potential threat posed in electoral terms by republican 'dissidents' did not transpire.

Election results

In terms of the election results, the DUP and Sinn Féin made further gains with a further squeeze on the more 'moderate' parties of the UUP and SDLP. The DUP and Sinn Féin cemented their position as the leading parties of their respective communities with thirty-six and twenty-eight Assembly seats, respectively. The DUP increased its share of the vote and number of Assembly seats, guaranteeing the post of First Minister and four ministries. Sinn Féin also increased its share of the vote and number of seats, thereby confirming the party's right to the post of Deputy First Minister and three ministries. The two 'moderate' parties fared badly: the UUP's share of Assembly seats plummeted from twenty-four to eighteen (eighteen seats behind the DUP) and the SDLP won just sixteen seats, qualifying for only one executive seat.

It was a good election for the Alliance Party who won an extra seat to seven Assembly seats and an increased share of the vote from 3.7 per cent in 2003 to 5.2 per cent. The party also celebrated the notable success of Anna Lo in South Belfast, the first Chinese person to be elected to a European legislature. Both unionist and republican dissidents failed to make much impact. The election was a resounding defeat for Robert McCartney who polled badly in the six constituencies he contested and even lost his own Assembly seat in North Down. In the wake of these poor results, McCartney announced that he would be leaving Northern Ireland politics. Republican dissidents also fared badly; it appears that Sinn Féin's public and private consultations on the direction of politics largely settled unease over the party's support for the police service.

Of additional note is that the DUP and Sinn Féin were also extremely competent in vote management and balancing the number of candidates to achieve the greatest share of seats in the respective constituencies. For instance, Sinn Féin contested five candidates in the West Belfast constituency and all five were elected, and in Mid-Ulster the party's three candidates were elected on the first count. The DUP displayed excellent vote management in Strangford with the election of four candidates and three candidates elected in East Belfast. The overall turnout was 62.87 per cent and, as at previous elections, there was a higher turnout in nationalist constituencies in the west than unionist constituencies in the east. The 108 elected candidates included thirty MLAs who were new to the Assembly and only eighteen women. Although the new Assembly included some high profile women such as Iris Robinson and Arlene Foster (DUP), Caitriona Ruane and Michelle Gildernew (Sinn Féin), Margaret Ritchie (SDLP) and Naomi Long (Alliance), Northern Ireland politics continued to deliver a lack of women coming through from candidature to winning seats.

Overall, the election created the conditions for a new political landscape in Northern Ireland, leading to the formation of a four-party power-sharing Executive. The election results meant that a new Executive would have a unionist majority: 7:5 unionist:nationalist including First Minister and Deputy First Minister. The new Assembly would have a combined DUP/UUP unionist total of fifty-four seats compared with a combined Sinn Féin/SDLP total of forty-four seats.

Return to power sharing

In the immediate aftermath of the election, it was still not clear whether the DUP would agree to share power with Sinn Féin. Time was running out as the parties had just two weeks to agree whether they would share power from 26 March 2007. For Secretary of State Peter Hain, the choice for the parties was 'devolution or dissolution' and the British Government would not seek to extend the deadline. By the end of the month, however, in circumstances where a deal seemed increasingly possible, the Secretary of State changed his threat to dissolution if parties failed to agree on a way forward, notably not a requirement for a functioning government. The parties set about securing a sufficiently substantial financial package in meetings with Tony Blair and the Chancellor Gordon Brown.

The DUP/Sinn Féin deal
On 24 March the DUP Executive endorsed the leadership's motion to enter a power-sharing government. Yet deadline day, 26 March 2007, passed without the restoration of the devolved institutions.

Table 8.4 'Indicative' allocation of portfolios under d'Hondt April 2007

Round	Party	Portfolio	Minister
1.	DUP	Finance and Personnel	Peter Robinson
2.	Sinn Féin	Education	Caitriona Ruane
3.	DUP	Enterprise, Trade and Investment	Nigel Dodds
4.	UUP	Health, Social Services and Public Safety	Michael McGimpsey
5.	SDLP	Social Development	Margaret Ritchie
6.	Sinn Féin	Regional Development	Conor Murphy
7.	DUP	Environment	Arlene Foster
8.	Sinn Féin	Agriculture and Rural Development	Michelle Gildernew
9.	DUP	Culture, Arts and Leisure	Edwin Poots
10.	UUP	Employment and Learning	Reg Empey

What transpired, however, was an extraordinary agreement between the DUP and Sinn Féin that devolution would be postponed for six weeks until 8 May. The quite remarkable image of Ian Paisley and Gerry Adams sitting side by side in Parliament Buildings, Stormont was broadcast around the world as a milestone in Northern Ireland's peace process. At the press conference both DUP leader Ian Paisley and Sinn Féin President Gerry Adams signalled their commitment to a return to devolution.

A remarkable series of events followed the agreement between the DUP and Sinn Féin. For instance, on 2 April, the four parties who would have ministerial positions in the new government ran an 'indicative' d'Hondt. On the basis of the parties' respective electoral strength, the DUP would have four seats, Sinn Féin three, the UUP two and the SDLP one. The parties chose their preferred portfolios and in the following days and weeks assigned ministers to those departments. Following the operation of d'Hondt the parties then set about meeting their departmental officials and conducted some preparatory work in advance of the transfer of power.

As per coalition formation in 29 November 1999, the new executive which took office on 8 May 2007 corresponds to a consociational 'grand coalition' in which society's main segments are represented in government.[9] One of the main critiques of consociationalism is that a grand coalition leaves an inadequate opposition in the legislature. Following the 2007 Northern Ireland Assembly election, nine-eight MLAs were members of governing parties with just ten MLAs from non-governing parties. Thus, the question arises as to what extent just ten MLAs would be able to provide an effective opposition to the four-party coalition. As per devolution in 1999–2002, however, the Assembly Committees have the potential to develop an effective opposition role.

A new Executive

Following the election and deal between the DUP and Sinn Féin there was some discussion as to what kind of power sharing might take place with these two parties occupying the top two posts of First Minister and Deputy First Minister, respectively. It is worth remembering that in 1998 the UUP and SDLP talked of 'accommodation' and 'reconciliation' between the two communities. As Chapter 7 illustrated, however, the operation of the Executive was nevertheless blighted by a lack of inter-party trust. Thus, the potential for a DUP/Sinn Féin-led coalition raised the question whether the new government would be prone to deadlock and stalemate. There was some speculation whether the administration would, as termed by Sinn Féin's Gerry Adams, be 'a battle a day'.

So, to what extent do the parties in the new Executive work together? How successful is the new Assembly? Is the administration more successful than that which operated 1999 to 2002? Of particular note is that a remarkable series of events took place before and after the opening of Stormont on 8 May 2007. In early April DUP leader Ian Paisley made a visit to Dublin, shook hands with Taoiseach Bertie Ahern for the first time and spoke of 'the prospect of mutual and respectful co-operation'. On 11 May Paisley and Ahern met at the site of the Battle of the Boyne in County Meath where, in 1690, Protestant Prince William of Orange defeated Catholic James II – a victory celebrated by unionists every year on 12 July.

The first public encounter between the First Minister (Designate) and Deputy First Minister (Designate) was a held at Stormont on 1 May at a visit from European Commission President Jose Barroso who pledged the formation of a taskforce to explore Northern Ireland's economic prospects. The DUP and Sinn Féin also joined forces to lobby the UK Chancellor Gordon Brown regarding a financial package for Northern Ireland. Brown pledged a £51 billion package for the new Executive, an amount which disappointed the parties as they claimed most of it had already been allocated to Northern Ireland. An all-party consensus also called on the British Government to delay the introduction of planned water charges which was arguably the main issue for the electorate in the run up to the election.

Despite the promising signs of a positive working relationship between Paisley and McGuinness and between all the governing parties more generally, the administration has not yet been tested. Indeed, a number of considerable challenges await the new Executive including post-primary education transfer arrangements, Irish lan-guage legislation and the Review of Public Administration. Of note is that the St Andrews Agreement stated that the British Government would introduce an Irish Language Act and 'work with the incoming Executive to enhance and protect the development of the Irish lan-guage'. At the time of writing, Executive decision making was not yet required on these issues. Significantly, the DUP chose the Department of Culture, Arts and Leisure under d'Hondt and stressed that it would veto any Irish language legislation. As these matters are particularly controversial, they are likely to test the amendments made by the St Andrews Agreement and the Northern Ireland (St Andrews Agreement) Act 2006.

Other early developments have included an attempt on the part of the Executive to present a collective inter-departmental response to the flooding crisis in June 2007. Activity has also taken place in rela-tion to north–south cooperation under Strand Two and east–west relations under Strand Three with meetings of the North–South Ministerial Council and the British–Irish Council in July 2007. The

NSMC meeting was held in Armagh and attended by ministers from the Northern Ireland Executive and the newly-formed coalition in the Irish Republic. The meeting was significant due to the participation of the DUP who boycotted the institution during the previous administration. Ministers from both jurisdictions agreed to spend £400 million on cross-border road projects including investment from Dublin. The BIC meeting was held at Stormont with representatives from across the UK and the Isle of Man, Guernsey and Jersey including new British Prime Minister Gordon Brown and Scottish First Minister Alex Salmond.

....

✓ **What you should have learnt from reading this chapter**

- In the post-suspension period efforts were made by the British and Irish Governments to restore devolution leading to the convening of inter-party talks and the publication of the St Andrews Agreement in October 2006.

- The political climate changed following DUP and Sinn Féin successes at the 2003 Assembly election, further cemented at the 2005 general election.

- The St Andrews Agreement made a number of important changes to the Good Friday/Belfast Agreement.

- The key issues leading up to the restoration of power sharing involved Sinn Féin's support for policing and the DUP's willingness to enter a new executive with republicans.

- The restoration of devolution followed an agreement between the DUP and Sinn Féin .

? **Likely examination question**

Discuss the significance of the St Andrews Agreement leading to the restoration of devolution in Northern Ireland in May 2007.

🖥 **Helpful websites**

Northern Ireland Assembly: http://www.niassembly.gov.uk

Northern Ireland Executive: http://www.northernireland.gov.uk

ARK Elections: http://www.ark.ac.uk/elections

Northern Ireland Life and Times Survey: http://www.ark.ac.uk/nilt

Suggestions for further reading

Arthur Aughey, *The Politics of Northern Ireland: Beyond the Belfast Agreement*, London: Routledge, 2005.

Jonathan Tonge, *The New Northern Irish Politics?*, Basingstoke: Palgrave Macmillan, 2005.

Notes

Introduction

1. The Agreement agreed among the parties on 10 April 1998 is often called the Good Friday Agreement or the Belfast Agreement. The book uses these terms interchangeably and also refers to the 1998 Agreement.

Chapter 1

1. Brendan O'Leary and John McGarry, *The Politics of Antagonism: Understanding Northern Ireland*, London: Athlone Press, 1993, p. 3.
2. John McGarry and Brendan O'Leary, *Explaining Northern Ireland: Broken Images*, Oxford: Blackwell Publishing, 1995, p. 212.
3. Anthony D. Smith, *National Identity*, London: Penguin, 1991, p. 9.
4. Walker Connor, *Ethnonationalism: The Quest for Understanding*, Princeton: Princeton University Press, 1994, p. 42.
5. Connor, *Ethnonationalism*, p. 46.
6. John Barry, 'National identities, historical narratives and patron states in Northern Ireland', in Michael Waller and Andrew Linklater (eds), *Political Loyalty and the Nation-State*, London: Routledge, 2003, p. 190.
7. Barry, *Political Loyalty*, p. 191.
8. Barry, *Political Loyalty*, p. 196.
9. Adrian Little, 'The problems of antagonism: applying liberal political theory to conflict in Northern Ireland', *British Journal of Politics and International Relations*, 2003, Vol. 5, No. 3, p. 374.
10. Little, 'The problems of antagonism', p. 377.
11. Little, 'The problems of antagonism', p. 387.
12. See Rick Wilford, 'Women, ethnicity and nationalism: surveying the ground', in Rick Wilford and Robert L. Miller (eds), *Women, Ethnicity and Nationalism: the Politics of Transition*, London: Routledge, 1998, pp. 1–22.
13. Elisabeth Porter, 'Identity, location, plurality: women, nationalism and Northern Ireland', in Rick Wilford and Robert Miller (eds), *Women, Ethnicity and Nationalism: the Politics of Transition*, London: Routledge, 1998, p. 37.
14. Elisabeth Porter, 'Identity, location, plurality', p. 40.

15. John McGarry and Brendan O'Leary, *Explaining Northern Ireland*, p. 355.
16. John Whyte, *Interpreting Northern Ireland*, Oxford: Clarendon Press, 1990, p. 91.
17. John McGarry and Brendan O'Leary, *Explaining Northern Ireland*, Ch. 2, pp. 62–91.
18. John Whyte, *Interpreting Northern Ireland*, p. 193.
19. John McGarry and Brendan O'Leary, *Explaining Northern Ireland*, p. 91.
20. John McGarry and Brendan O'Leary, *Explaining Northern Ireland*, p. 364.
21. Jonathan Tonge, *Northern Ireland*, Cambridge: Polity Press, 2006, p. 14.
22. Jonathan Tonge, *Northern Ireland*, p. 17.
23. Arend Lijphart, *Democracy in Plural Societies: A Comparative Exploration*, New Haven: Yale University Press, 1977, p. 1.
24. Rick Wilford, 'Inverting consociationalism? Policy, pluralism and the post-modern', in Brigid Hadfield (ed.), *Northern Ireland: Politics and the Constitution*, Buckingham: Open University Press, 1992, p. 31.
25. Rupert Taylor, 'Northern Ireland: consociation or social transformation?', in John McGarry (ed.), *Northern Ireland and the Divided World*, Oxford: Oxford University Press, 2001, p. 38.
26. Donald L. Horowitz, 'The Northern Ireland Agreement: clear, consociational and risky', in John McGarry (ed.), *Northern Ireland and the Divided World: Post-Agreement Northern Ireland in Comparative Perspective*, Oxford: Oxford University Press, 2001, p. 92.
27. Donald L. Horowitz, 'The Northern Ireland Agreement', p. 93.
28. John McGarry and Brendan O'Leary, *The Northern Ireland Conflict: Consociational Engagements*, Oxford: Oxford University Press, 2004, pp. 25–6.
29. John McGarry and Brendan O'Leary, *The Northern Ireland Conflict*, pp. 35–6.

Chapter 2

1. Brendan O'Leary and John McGarry, *The Politics of Antagonism: Understanding Northern Ireland*, London: Athlone Press, 1993, pp. 69–70.
2. Brendan O'Leary and John McGarry, *The Politics of Antagonism*, p. 74.
3. Brendan O'Leary and John McGarry, *The Politics of Antagonism*, p. 100.
4. Paul Bew, Peter Gibbon, and Henry Patterson, *Northern Ireland 1921/2001 Political Forces and Social Classes*, London: Serif, 2002, p. 4.

5. Paul Bew, Peter Gibbon, and Henry Patterson, *Northern Ireland 1921/2001*, p. 9.
6. Brendan O'Leary and John McGarry, *The Politics of Antagonism*, p. 114.
7. Brendan O'Leary and John McGarry, *The Politics of Antagonism*, p. 147.
8. Paul Dixon, *Northern Ireland: The Politics of War and Peace*, Basingstoke: Palgrave, 2001, p. 58.
9. Brendan O'Leary and John McGarry, *The Politics of Antagonism*, p. 163.
10. Brendan O'Leary and John McGarry, *The Politics of Antagonism*, p. 157.
11. Paul Dixon, *Northern Ireland*, 2001.
12. Richard English, *Armed Struggle: The History of the IRA*, Basingstoke: Macmillan, 2003, p. 96.
13. Paul Dixon, *Northern Ireland*, p. 86.
14. Richard English, *Armed Struggle*, p. 99.
15. Paul Dixon, *Northern Ireland*, p. 78.
16. Richard English, *Armed Struggle*, pp. 90–4.
17. The Provisional IRA will be referred to as the IRA throughout the remainder of this book.
18. Richard English, *Armed Struggle*, p. 107.
19. Richard English, *Armed Struggle*, pp. 120–5.
20. Brendan O'Leary and John McGarry, *The Politics of Antagonism: Understanding Northern Ireland*, London: Athlone Press, 1993, p. 176.
21. A tribunal into the events of 'Bloody Sunday' was set up by the Blair Government in 1998. Overseen by Lord Saville, the tribunal heard evidence from 921 witnesses and ended in 2004. The tribunal is expected to publish its report in 2008.
22. Northern Ireland Council for Integrated Education: http://www.nicie.org.
23. http://www.asharedfutureni.gov.uk.
24. Dominic Bryan, *Orange Parades: The Politics of Ritual, Tradition and Control*, London: Pluto Press, 2000, pp. 100–9.

Chapter 3

1. Paul Mitchell and Rick Wilford, *Politics in Northern Ireland*, Oxford: Westview Press, 1999, p. 108.
2. Christopher Farrington, *Ulster Unionism and the Peace Process in Northern Ireland*, Basingstoke: Palgrave Macmillan, 2006, p. 83.
3. Paul Mitchell and Rick Wilford, *Politics in Northern Ireland*, p. 109.
4. Christopher Farrington, *Ulster Unionism*, p. 64.

5. Christopher Farrington, *Ulster Unionism*, p. 148.
6. Feargal Cochrane, *Unionist Politics and the Politics of Unionism since the Anglo-Irish Agreement*, Cork: Cork University Press, 2001, p. 93.
7. Steve Bruce, *God Save Ulster! The Religion and Politics of Paisleyism*, Oxford: Oxford University Press, 1986, p. 51.
8. Steve Bruce, *God Save Ulster!*, p. 249.
9. Steve Bruce, *God Save Ulster!*.
10. Feargal Cochrane, *Unionist Politics and the Politics of Unionism*, p. 46.
11. Steve Bruce, *God Save Ulster!*, p. 89.
12. Steve Bruce, *God Save Ulster!*, p. 9.
13. Gerard Murray, *John Hume and the SDLP: Impact and Survival in Northern Ireland*, Dublin: Irish Academic Press, 1998, p. 39.
14. Gerard Murray, *John Hume*, pp. 92–4.
15. Gerard Murray, *John Hume*, p. 77.
16. Gerard Murray, *John Hume*, p. 135.
17. Gerard Murray, *John Hume*, p. 263.
18. Richard English, *Armed Struggle: The History of the IRA*, Basingstoke: Macmillan, 2003, p. 107. (Original emphasis.)
19. Richard English, *Armed Struggle*, p. 254.
20. Gerard Murray and Jonathan Tonge, *Sinn Féin and the SDLP: From Alienation to Participation*, Dublin: O'Brien Press, 2005, p. 33.
21. Richard English, *Armed Struggle*, p. 244.
22. Richard English, *Armed Struggle*, p. 265.
23. Richard English, *Armed Struggle*, p. 271.
24. Richard English, *Armed Struggle*, p. 299.
25. Henry Patterson, *Ireland Since 1939*, Dublin: Penguin Ireland, 2006, p. 341.
26. Paul Mitchell and Rick Wilford, *Politics in Northern Ireland*, p. 101.
27. Richard English, *Armed Struggle*, p. 121.
28. Richard English, *Armed Struggle*, p. 378.
29. For reports of the Independent Monitoring Commission see http://www.independentmonitoringcommission.org.
30. Richard English, *Armed Struggle*, p. 316.

Chapter 4

1. Paul Bew, Peter Gibbon and Henry Patterson, *Northern Ireland 1921/2001 Political Forces and Social Classes*, London: Serif, 2002, p. 160.

2. Paul Bew, Peter Gibbon and Henry Patterson, *Northern Ireland 1921/2001*.

3. Henry Patterson, *Ireland Since 1939*, Dublin: Penguin Ireland, 2006, p. 225.

4. Paul Bew, Peter Gibbon and Henry Patterson, *Northern Ireland 1921/2001*, p. 187.

5. Henry Patterson, *Ireland Since 1939*, p. 239.

6. Henry Patterson, *Ireland Since 1939*, p. 240.

7. Henry Patterson, *Ireland Since 1939*, p. 242.

8. See http://www.ark.ac.uk/elections.

9. Paul Bew, Peter Gibbon and Henry Patterson, *Northern Ireland 1921/2001*, p. 202.

10. Paul Bew, Peter Gibbon and Henry Patterson, *Northern Ireland 1921/2001*, p. 202.

11. Feargal Cochrane, *Unionist Politics and the Politics of Unionism since the Anglo-Irish Agreement*, Cork: Cork University Press, 2001, p. 31.

12. Gerard Murray and Jonathan Tonge, *Sinn Féin and the SDLP: From Alienation to Participation*, Dublin: O'Brien Press, 2005, p. 139.

13. Gerard Murray and Jonathan Tonge, *Sinn Féin and the SDLP*, p. 150.

14. John McGarry and Brendan O'Leary, *Explaining Northern Ireland: Broken Images*, Oxford: Blackwell, 1995, p. 48.

15. Feargal Cochrane, *Unionist Politics*, p. 279.

16. Paul Bew, Peter Gibbon and Henry Patterson, *Northern Ireland 1921/2001*, p. 212.

17. Gerard Murray and Jonathan Tonge, *Sinn Féin and the SDLP*, pp. 177–8.

18. Paul Bew, Peter Gibbon and Henry Patterson, *Northern Ireland 1921/2001*, p. 220.

19. See Brooke's speech at Conflict Archive on the Internet: http://cain.ulst.ac.uk.

20. Joint Declaration on Peace: The Downing Street Declaration, 15 December 1993, available at http://cain.ulst.ac.uk.

21. Thomas Hennessey, *The Northern Ireland Peace Process: Ending the Troubles?*, Dublin: Gill and Macmillan, 2000, p. 81.

22. Thomas Hennessey, *The Northern Ireland Peace Process*, p. 84.

23. Thomas Hennessey, *The Northern Ireland Peace Process*, p. 82.

24. Thomas Hennessey, *The Northern Ireland Peace Process*, p. 90.

25. Gerard Murray and Jonathan Tonge, *Sinn Féin and the SDLP*, p. 189.

Chapter 5

1. John McGarry and Brendan O'Leary, *Explaining Northern Ireland: Broken Images*, Oxford: Blackwell, 1995, p. 29.
2. John McGarry and Brendan O'Leary, *Explaining Northern Ireland*, p. 57.
3. Gerard Murray and Jonathan Tonge, *Sinn Féin and the SDLP: From Alienation to Participation*, Dublin: O'Brien Press, 2005, p. 139.
4. See 'Hume–Adams' document at http://cain.ulst.ac.uk.
5. Gerard Murray and Jonathan Tonge, *Sinn Féin and the SDLP*, p. 182.
6. John McGarry and Brendan O'Leary, *Explaining Northern Ireland*, p. 45.
7. John McGarry and Brendan O'Leary, *Explaining Northern Ireland*.
8. Paul Bew, Peter Gibbon and Henry Patterson, *Northern Ireland 1921/2001 Political Forces and Social Classes*, London: Serif, 2002, p. 157.
9. *The Guardian*, 14 March 2007.
10. John McGarry and Brendan O'Leary, *Explaining Northern Ireland*, p. 387.
11. Thomas Hennessey, *The Northern Ireland Peace Process: Ending the Troubles?*, Dublin: Gill and Macmillan, 2000, p. 67.
12. Richard English, *Armed Struggle: The History of the IRA*, Basingstoke: Macmillan, 2003, p. 269.
13. Thomas Hennessey, *The Northern Ireland Peace Process*, p. 74.
14. *The Guardian*, 14 March 2007.
15. *The Guardian*, 14 March 2007.
16. Catherine O'Donnell, *Fianna Fail, Irish Republicanism and the Northern Ireland Troubles 1968–2005*, Dublin: Irish Academic Press, 2007, p. xiv.
17. Catherine O'Donnell, *Fianna Fail*, p. xvii.
18. Thomas Hennessey, *The Northern Ireland Peace Process*, p. 107.
19. Catherine O'Donnell, *Fianna Fail*, p. 58.
20. Thomas Hennessey, *The Northern Ireland Peace Process*, pp. 38–48.
21. Catherine O'Donnell, *Fianna Fail*, pp. 54–6.
22. Catherine O'Donnell, *Fianna Fail*, pp. 72–3.
23. Catherine O'Donnell, *Fianna Fail*, p. 30.
24. Catherine O'Donnell, *Fianna Fail*, p. 63.
25. Thomas Hennessey, *The Northern Ireland Peace Process*, pp. 106–7.
26. *Belfast Telegraph*, 11 March 2007.
27. *Irish Times*, 5 April 2007.
28. See Paul Arthur, *Special Relationships: Britain, Ireland and the Northern Ireland Problem*, Belfast: Blackstaff Press, 2000.

29. *The Guardian*, 27 March 2007.
30. *Irish Times*, 17 March 2007.

Chapter 6

1. Richard English, *Armed Struggle: The History of the IRA*, Basingstoke: Macmillan, 2003, p. 325.
2. Richard English, *Armed Struggle*, p. 326.
3. Thomas Hennessey, *The Northern Ireland Peace Process: Ending the Troubles?*, Dublin: Gill and Macmillan, 2000, p. 100.
4. http://cain.ulst.ac.uk.
5. http://cain.ulst.ac.uk.
6. Richard English, *Armed Struggle*, p. 289.
7. http://www.ark.ac.uk/elections.
8. Gerard Murray and Jonathan Tonge, *Sinn Féin and the SDLP: From Alienation to Participation*, Dublin: O'Brien Press, 2005, p. 193.
9. Thomas Hennessey, *The Northern Ireland Peace Process*, p. 104.
10. Thomas Hennessey, *The Northern Ireland Peace Process*, p. 105.
11. Thomas Hennessey, *The Northern Ireland Peace Process*, p. 108.
12. http://cain.ulst.ac.uk.
13. Joseph Ruane and Jennifer Todd (eds), *After the Good Friday Agreement: Analysing Political Change in Northern Ireland*, Dublin: University College Dublin Press, 1999, p. vii.
14. http://cain.ulst.ac.uk.
15. Paul Arthur, *Special Relationships: Britain, Ireland and the Northern Ireland Problem*, Belfast: Blackstaff Press, 2000, p. 248.
16. Brendan O'Leary, 'The nature of the Agreement', *Fordham International Law Journal*, 1999, 22, 4, p. 1649.
17. Donald L. Horowitz, 'Explaining the Northern Ireland Agreement: the sources of an unlikely constitutional consensus', *British Journal of Political Science*, 2002, 32, p. 194.
18. Donald L. Horowitz, 'Explaining the Northern Ireland Agreement', p. 215.
19. *News Letter*, 12 April 1998.
20. Arthur Aughey, 'The 1998 Agreement: unionist responses', in Michael Cox, Adrian Guelke and Fiona Stephen (eds), *A Farewell to Arms? From 'Long War' to Long Peace in Northern Ireland*, Manchester: Manchester University Press, 2000.

21. http://cain.ulst.ac.uk.
22. Gerry Adams, *Hope and History: Making Peace in Ireland*, London: Mounteagle, 2003, pp. 367–8.
23. Gerard Murray and Jonathan Tonge, *Sinn Féin and the SDLP: From Alienation to Participation*, 2005, p. 200.
24. Gerard Murray and Jonathan Tonge, *Sinn Féin and the SDLP*, p. 202.
25. http://cain.ulst.ac.uk.
26. *Irish Times*, 17 November 1998.
27. *Sunday Tribune*, 12 April 1998.

Chapter 7

1. Derek Birrell, 'Northern Ireland business in Parliament: the impact of the suspension of devolution in 2002', *Parliamentary Affairs*, 2007, 60, 2, 297–312, p. 304.
2. Jonathan Tonge, *The New Northern Irish Politics?*, Basingstoke: Palgrave Macmillan, 2005, p. 136.
3. Arend Lijphart, *Democracy in Plural Societies: A Comparative Exploration*, New Haven: Yale University Press, 1977, p. 25.
4. Arend Lijphart, *Democracy in Plural Societies*, p. 39.
5. Brendan O'Leary, 'The nature of the Agreement', *Fordham International Law Journal*, 1999, 22, 4, p. 1631.
6. Thomas Hennessey, *The Northern Ireland Peace Process: Ending the Troubles?*, Dublin: Gill and Macmillan, 2000, pp. 160–8.
7. Graham Walker, 'The British–Irish Council', in Rick Wilford (ed.), *Aspects of the Belfast Agreement*, Oxford: Oxford University Press, 2001, p. 130.
8. Graham Walker, 'The British–Irish Council', p. 129.
9. Jonathan Tonge, *The New Northern Irish Politics?*, p. 126.
10. The Agreement: Agreement reached in the multi-party negotiations, 10 April 1998, available at: http://www.nio.gov.uk/the-agreement.
11. See IRA statements at: http://news.bbc.co.uk/2/hi/uk_news/northern_ireland/4607913.stm.
12. http://news.bbc.co.uk/2/hi/uk_news/northern_ireland/4607913.stm.
13. See IICD statements at: http://cain.ulst.ac.uk/events/peace/decommission/iicdreports.htm.
14. The Agreement: Agreement reached in the multi-party negotiations, 10 April 1998, available at: http://www.nio.gov.uk/the-agreement.

15. Independent Commission on Policing in Northern Ireland, *A New Beginning: Policing in Northern Ireland – The Report of the Independent Commission on Policing in Northern Ireland*, Belfast, 9 September 1999, available at: http://cain.ulst.ac.uk/issues/police/police.htm.

Chapter 8

1. Joint Declaration by the British and Irish Governments, April 2003, available at: http://cain.ulst.ac.uk.
2. Jonathan Tonge, *The New Northern Irish Politics?*, Basingstoke: Palgrave Macmillan, 2005, p. 147.
3. Jonathan Tonge, *The New Northern Irish Politics?*, p. 148.
4. http://www.ark.ac.uk/nilt/2003/Political_Attitudes/index.html.
5. The Agreement: Agreement reached in the multi-party negotiations, 10 April 1998, available at: http://www.nio.gov.uk/the-agreement.
6. For IICD statements see http://cain.ulst.ac.uk.
7. British and Irish Governments' Agreement at St Andrews is available at: www.nio.gov.uk.
8. www.nio.gov.uk.
9. Arend Lijphart, *Democracy in Plural Societies: A Comparative Exploration*, New Haven: Yale University Press, 1977, p. 25.

Bibliography

Gerry Adams, *Hope and History: Making Peace in Ireland*, London: Mounteagle, 2003.

Paul Arthur, *Special Relationships: Britain, Ireland and the Northern Ireland Problem*, Belfast: Blackstaff Press, 2000.

Arthur Aughey, 'The 1998 Agreement: unionist responses', in Michael Cox, Adrian Guelke, and Fiona Stephen (eds), *A Farewell to Arms? From 'Long War' to Long Peace in Northern Ireland*, Manchester: Manchester University Press, 2000.

John Barry, 'National identities, historical narratives and patron states in Northern Ireland', in Michael Waller and Andrew Linklater (eds), *Political Loyalty and the Nation-State*, London: Routledge, 2003.

Paul Bew, Peter Gibbon and Henry Patterson, *Northern Ireland 1921/2001 Political Forces and Social Classes*, London: Serif, 2002.

Derek Birrell, 'Northern Ireland business in Parliament: the impact of the suspension of devolution in 2002', *Parliamentary Affairs*, 2007, 60, 2, 297–312.

Steve Bruce, *God Save Ulster! The Religion and Politics of Paisleyism*, Oxford: Oxford University Press, 1986.

Dominic Bryan, *Orange Parades: The Politics of Ritual, Tradition and Control*, London: Pluto Press, 2000.

Feargal Cochrane, *Unionist Politics and the Politics of Unionism since the Anglo-Irish Agreement*, Cork: Cork University Press, 2001.

Walker Connor, *Ethnonationalism: The Quest for Understanding*, Princeton: Princeton University Press, 1994.

Paul Dixon, *Northern Ireland: The Politics of War and Peace*, Basingstoke: Palgrave, 2001.

Richard English, *Armed Struggle: The History of the IRA*, Basingstoke: Macmillan, 2003.

Christopher Farrington, *Ulster Unionism and the Peace Process in Northern Ireland*, Basingstoke: Palgrave Macmillan, 2006.

Thomas Hennessey, *A History of Northern Ireland 1920–1996*, Dublin: Gill and Macmillan, 1997.

Thomas Hennessey, *The Northern Ireland Peace Process: Ending the Troubles?*, Dublin: Gill and Macmillan, 2000.

Donald L. Horowitz, 'The Northern Ireland Agreement: clear, consociational and risky', in John McGarry (ed.), *Northern Ireland and the Divided World: Post-Agreement Northern Ireland in Comparative Perspective*, Oxford: Oxford University Press, 2001.

Donald L. Horowitz, 'Explaining the Northern Ireland Agreement: the sources of an unlikely constitutional consensus', *British Journal of Political Science*, 2002, 32, 193–220.

Arend Lijphart, *Democracy in Plural Societies: A Comparative Exploration*, New Haven: Yale University Press, 1977.

Adrian Little, 'The problems of antagonism: applying liberal political theory to conflict in Northern Ireland', *British Journal of Politics and International Relations*, 2003, 5, 3, 373–92.

John McGarry and Brendan O'Leary, *Explaining Northern Ireland: Broken Images*, Oxford: Blackwell Publishing, 1995.

John McGarry and Brendan O' Leary, The Northern Ireland Conflict: Consociational Engagements, Oxford: Oxford University Press, 2004.

Paul Mitchell and Rick Wilford, *Politics in Northern Ireland*, Oxford: Westview Press, 1999.

Gerard Murray, *John Hume and the SDLP: Impact and Survival in Northern Ireland*, Dublin: Irish Academic Press, 1998.

Gerard Murray and Jonathan Tonge, *Sinn Féin and the SDLP: From Alienation to Participation*, Dublin: O'Brien Press, 2005.

Catherine O'Donnell, *Fianna Fail, Irish Republicanism and the Northern Ireland Troubles 1968–2005*, Dublin: Irish Academic Press, 2007.

Brendan O'Leary, 'The nature of the Agreement', *Fordham International Law Journal*, 1999, 22, 4, 1628–67.

Brendan O'Leary and John McGarry, *The Politics of Antagonism: Understanding Northern Ireland*, London: Athlone Press, 1993.

Henry Patterson, *Ireland Since 1939*, Dublin: Penguin Ireland, 2006.

Joseph Ruane and Jennifer Todd (eds), *After the Good Friday Agreement: Analysing Political Change in Northern Ireland*, Dublin: University College Dublin Press, 1999.

Anthony D. Smith, *National Identity*, London: Penguin, 1991.

Rupert Taylor, 'Northern Ireland: consociation or social transformation?', in John McGarry (ed.), *Northern Ireland and the Divided World: Post-Agreement Northern Ireland in Comparative Perspective*, Oxford: Oxford University Press, 2001.

Jonathan Tonge, *The New Northern Irish Politics?*, Basingstoke: Palgrave Macmillan, 2005.

Jonathan Tonge, *Northern Ireland*, Cambridge: Polity Press, 2006.

Graham Walker, 'The British–Irish Council', in Rick Wilford (ed.), *Aspects of the Belfast Agreement*, Oxford: Oxford University Press, 2001.

John Whyte, *Interpreting Northern Ireland*, Oxford: Clarendon Press, 1990.

Rick Wilford, 'Inverting consociationalism? Policy, pluralism and the post-modern', in Brigid Hadfield (ed.), *Northern Ireland: Politics and the Constitution*, Buckingham: Open University Press, 1992.

Rick Wilford and Robert L. Miller (eds), *Women, Ethnicity and Nationalism: the Politics of Transition*, London: Routledge, 1998.

Rick Wilford (ed.), *Aspects of the Belfast Agreement*, Oxford: Oxford University Press, 2001.

Index

Bold indicates that the term is defined